I0469071

Brantford Ontario and Area in Photos, Saving Our History One Photo at a Time

Photography
by Barbara Raué
2012

Series Name:
Cruising Ontario

Book 18: Brantford

Cover photo: Brantford House at #74

Series Name: Cruising Ontario

Book 1: London
Book 2: Dundas
Book 3: Hamilton
Book 4: Oakville
Book 5: Chesley
Book 6: Stoney Creek
Book 7: Waterdown
Book 8: Owen Sound
Book 9: Mount Forest
Book 10: Dundalk
Book 11: Burford and Area
Book 12: Waterford and Area
Book 13: Drumbo and Area
Book 14: Sheffield and Area
Book 15: Tavistock and Area
Book 16: Ancaster and Mount Hope
Book 17: Innerkip
Book 18: Brantford
Book 19: Burlington

Other Books by Barbara Raue

Coins of Gold

Arrows, Indians and Love

The Life and Times of Barbara
Volume 1: Inventions That Have Enhanced My Life
Volume 2: Entertainment That I Have Enjoyed
Volume 3: East Coast Trips
Volume 4: Olympics
Volume 5: Wonders of the World
Volume 6: Caribbean Cruises

Brantford

Brantford is a city located on the Grand River in Southern Ontario. Brantford is connected to Woodstock in the west and Hamilton in the east by Highway 403 and to Cambridge to the north and Simcoe to the south by Highway 24. Brantford is known by the nickname *The Telephone City* as former city resident Alexander Graham Bell conducted the first distant telephone call from the community to Paris, Ontario in 1876. It is also the birthplace of hockey player Wayne Gretzky.

Bethel Road

Bethel Road is located south of Highway 403, northwest of Brantford and south of Paris.

Falkland

Falkland is located on Falkland Road and King Edward Street, west of Paris, southeast of Etonia.

Eastwood

Captain Drew named it Eastwood Park, from which is derived Eastwood Village. Eastwood is west of Woodstock on Dundas Street, and east of Highway 401.

Etonia

Etonia is located on Governors and Canning Roads, north of Highway 403, west of Paris.

Gobles

In 1855 Gobles Corners was named after the late William L. Goble, son of Rev. Jacob Goble, who came to Canada from New York State in 1823. When the railway was built the station bore the name "Gobles".

Shakespeare

This tiny village located on Highway 7 and 8 between New Hamburg and Stratford was known as Bell's Corners after David Bell who founded the village. In 1852, the name was changed to Shakespeare.

Brantford

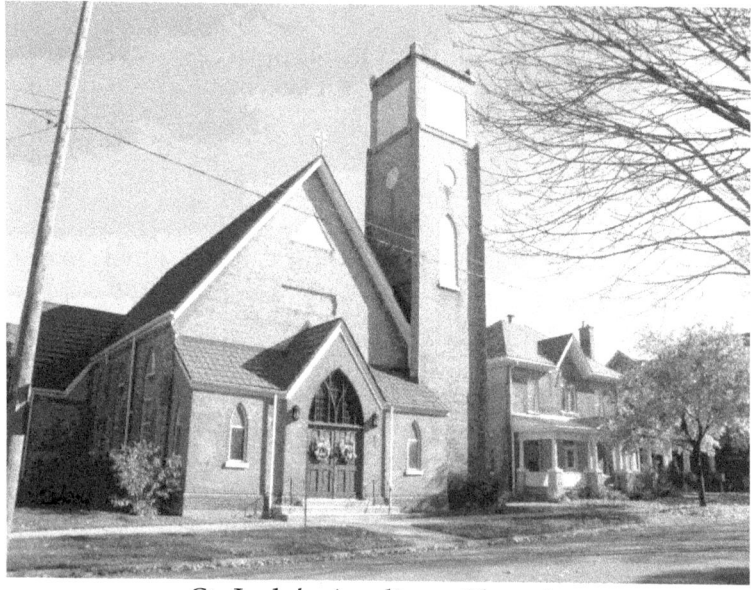

St. Jude's Anglican Church

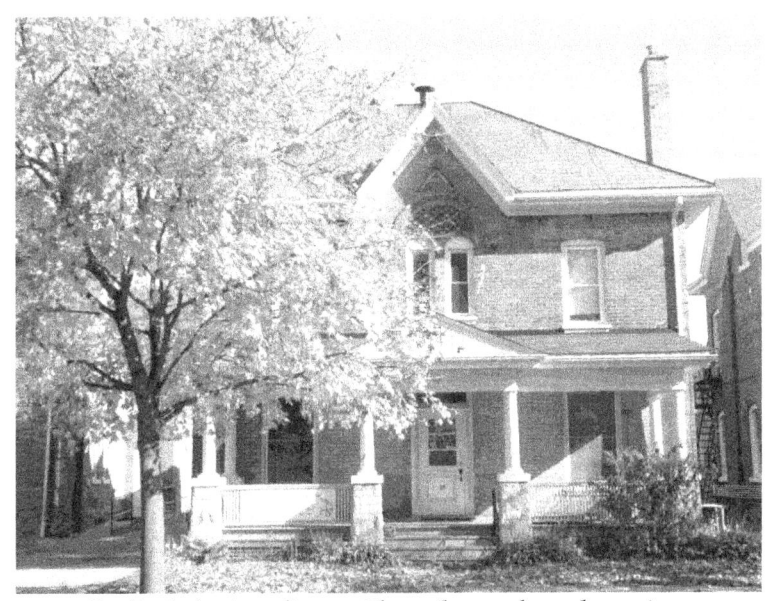

St. Jude's Anglican Church student housing
Centre gable Gothic Revival cottage

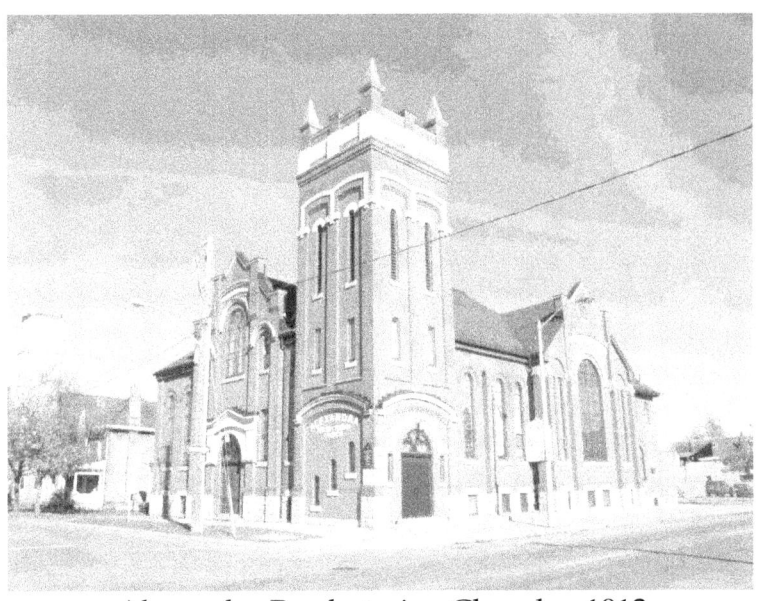

Alexandra Presbyterian Church – 1912

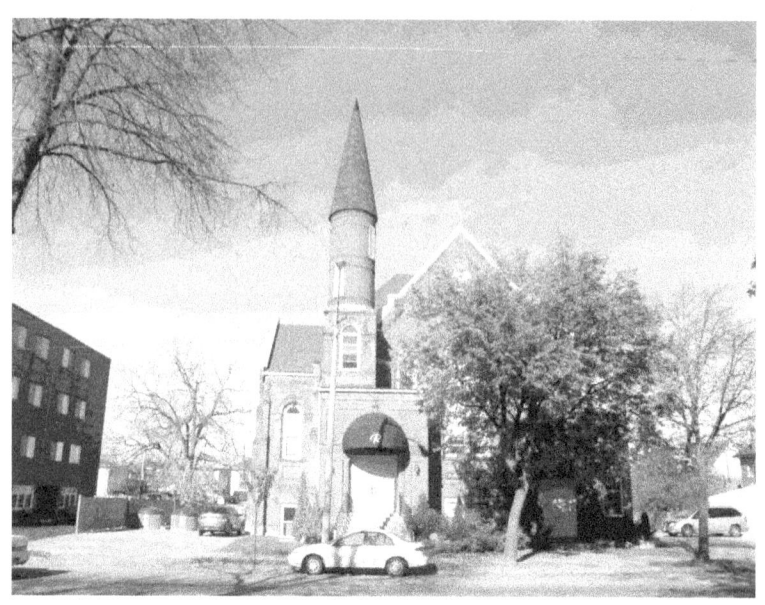

Calvary Baptist Church

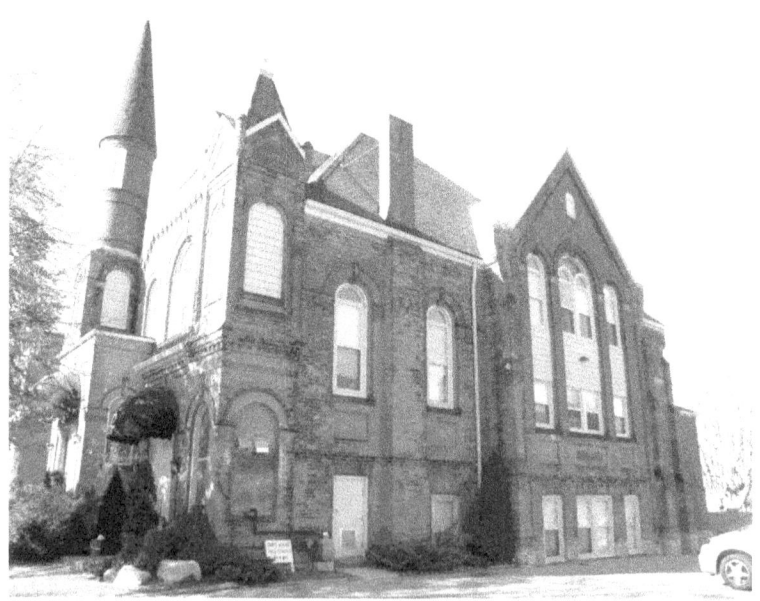

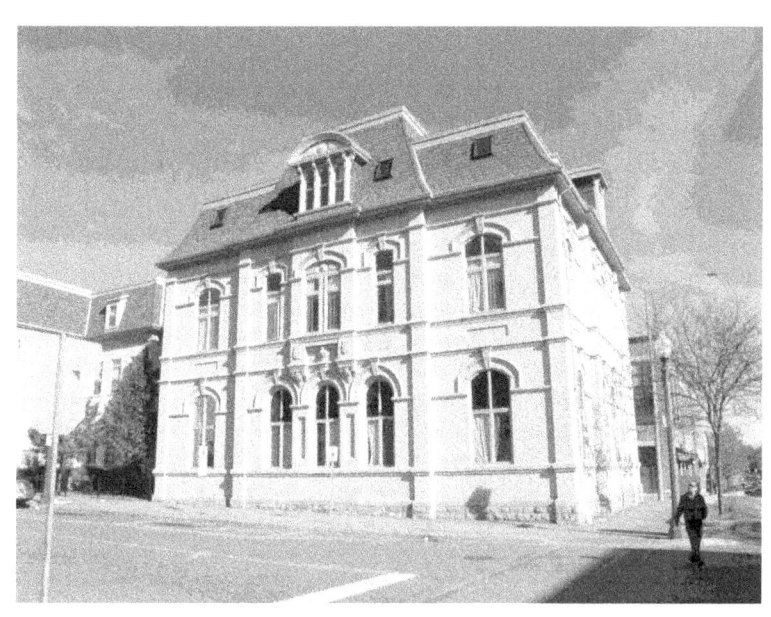

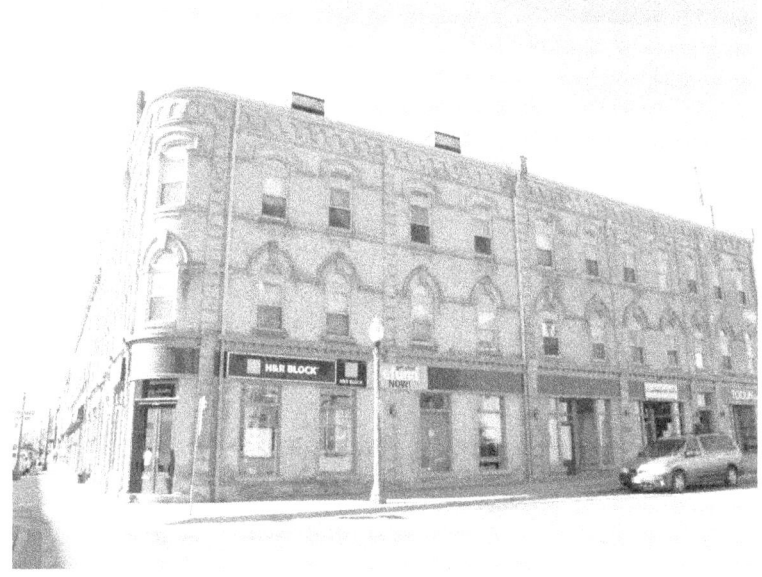

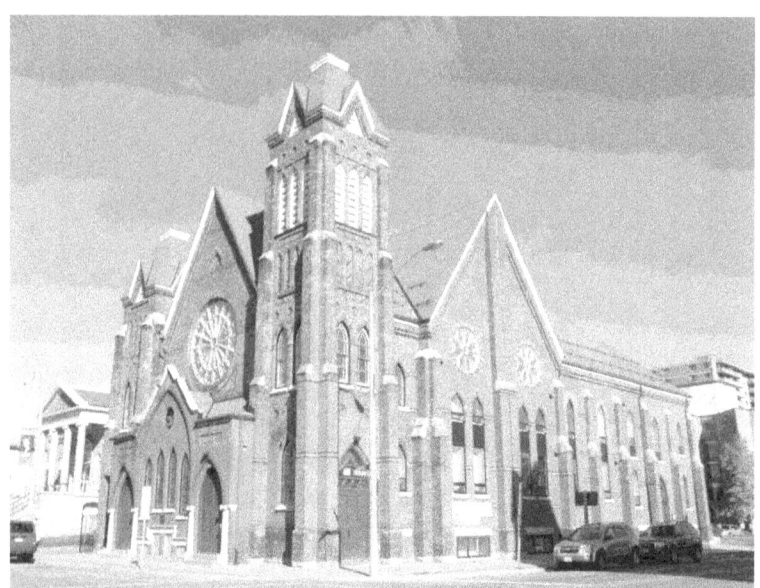

Church on the corner of Darling and George Streets
Built circa 1870 – now student housing

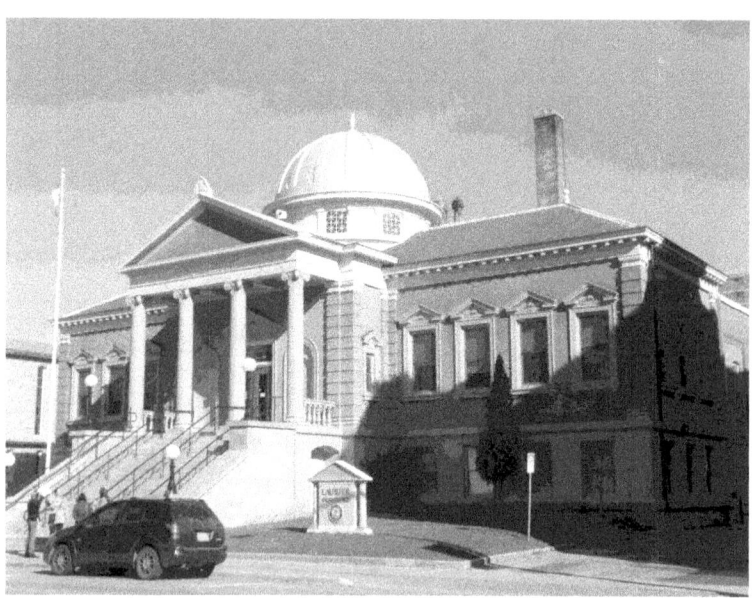

Laurier Brantford

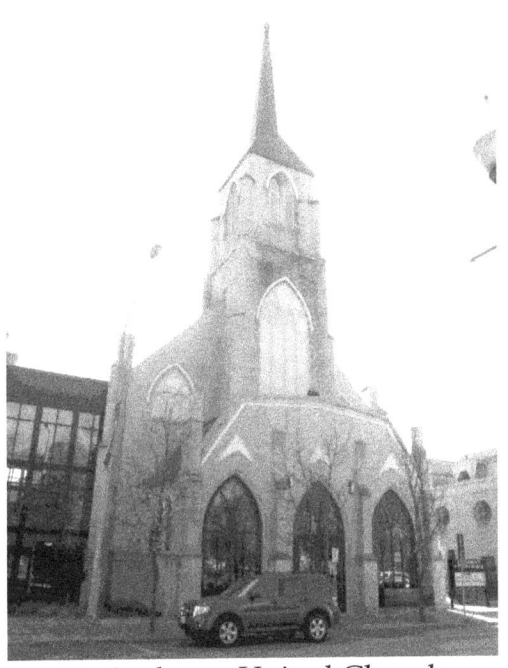

St. Andrews United Church

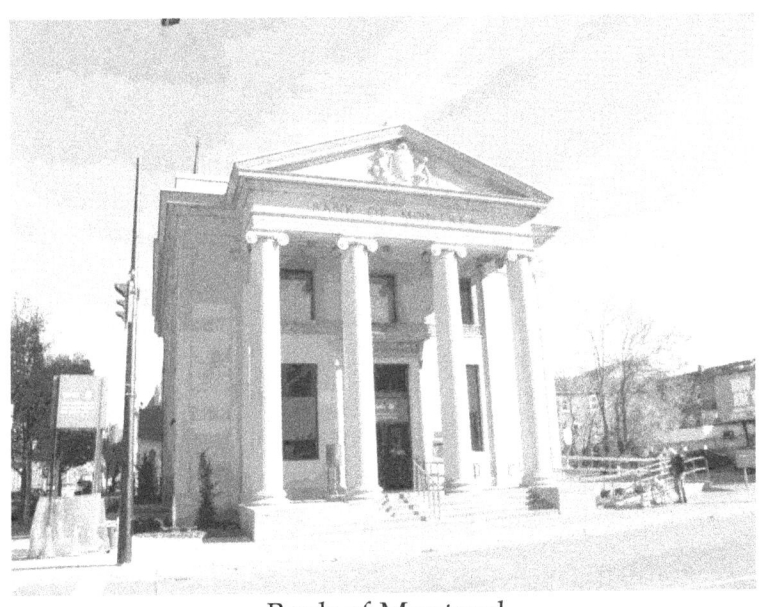

Bank of Montreal

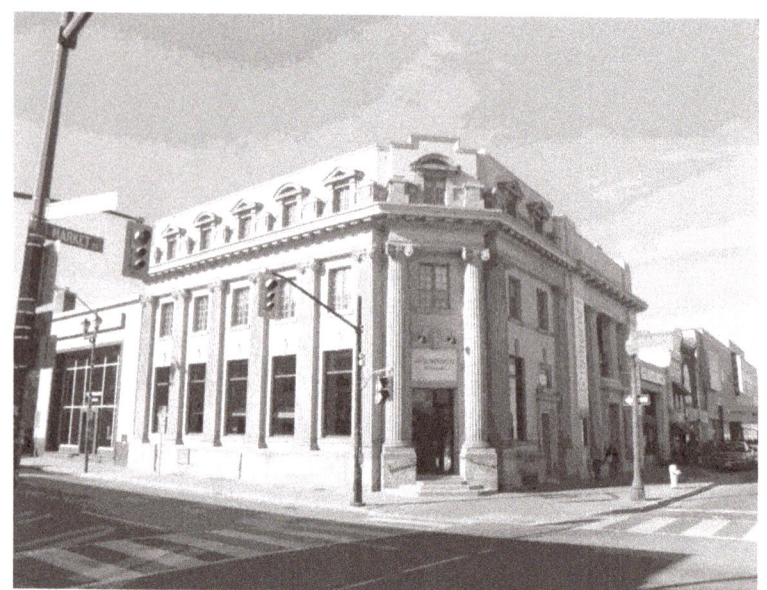

SC Johnson Building – corner Dalhousie & Market Streets

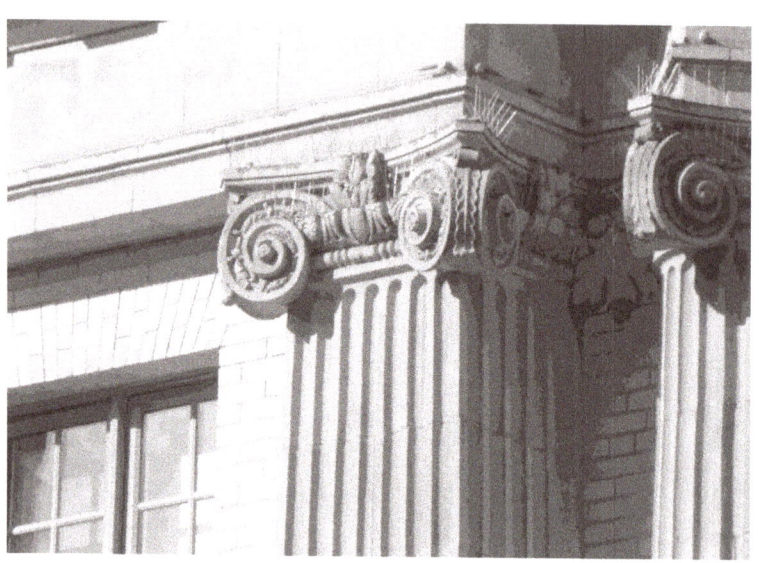

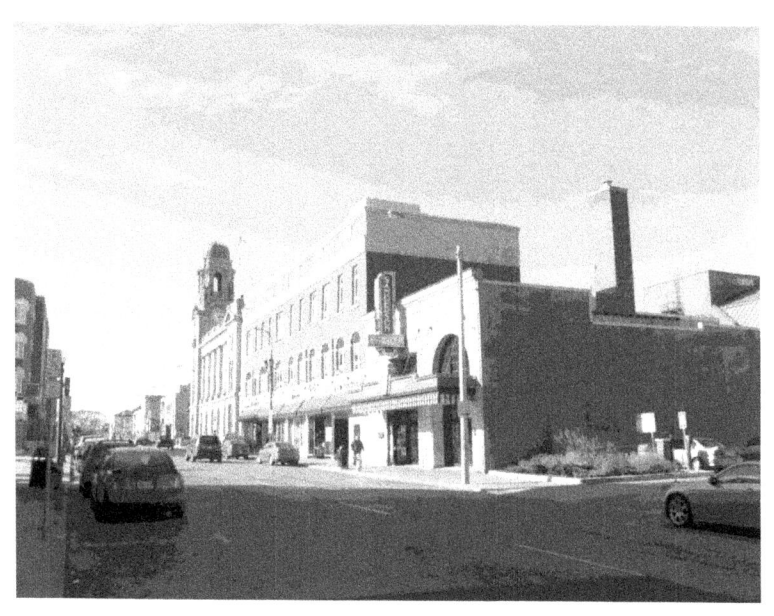

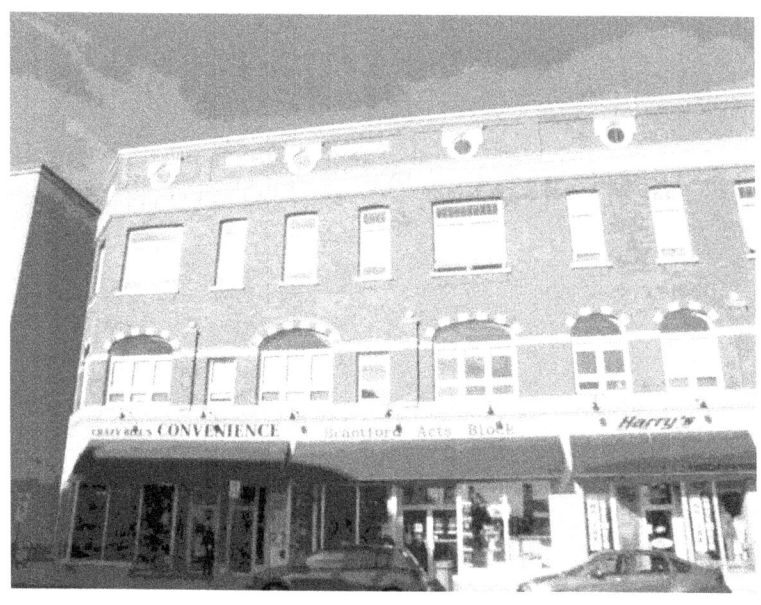

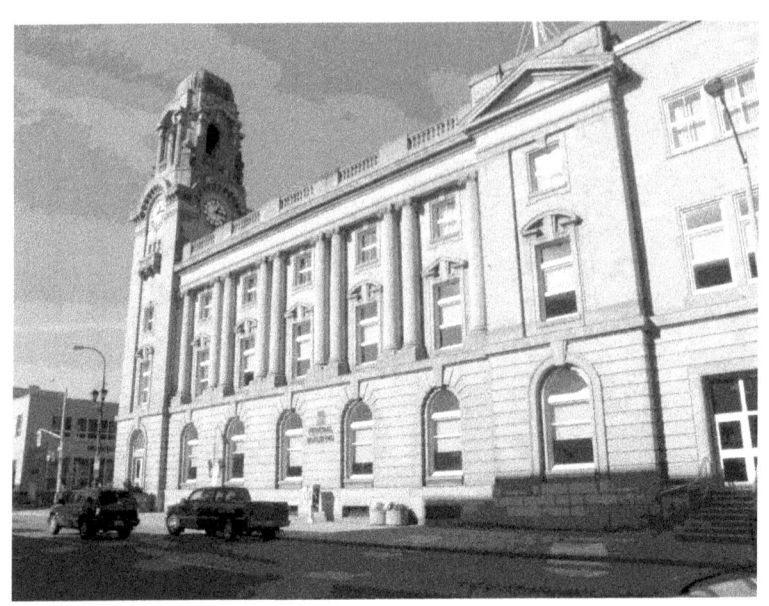

Federal Building – erected 1913

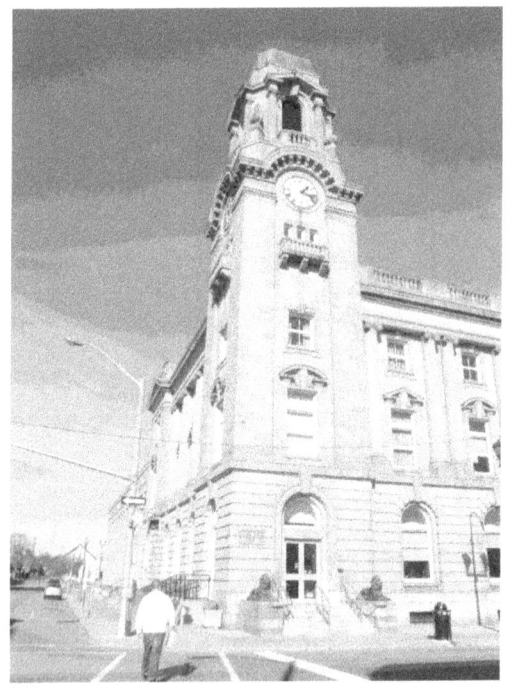

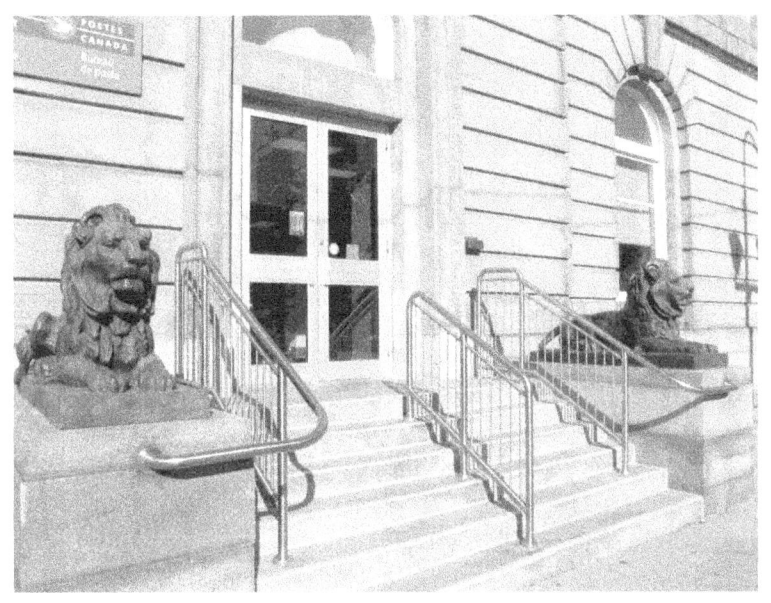

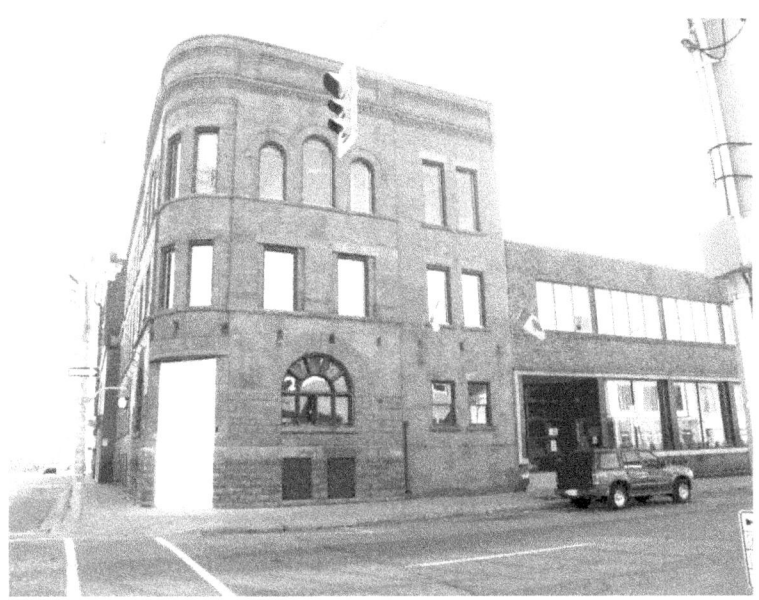

Expositor Building

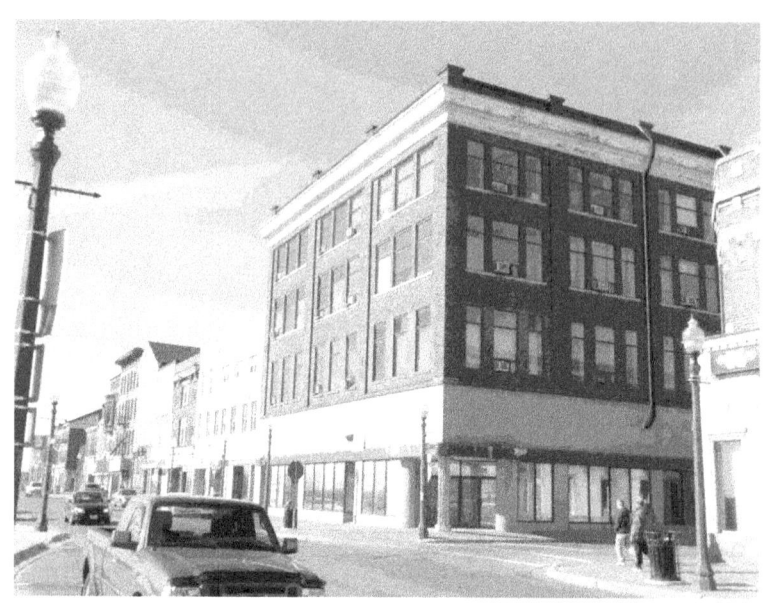

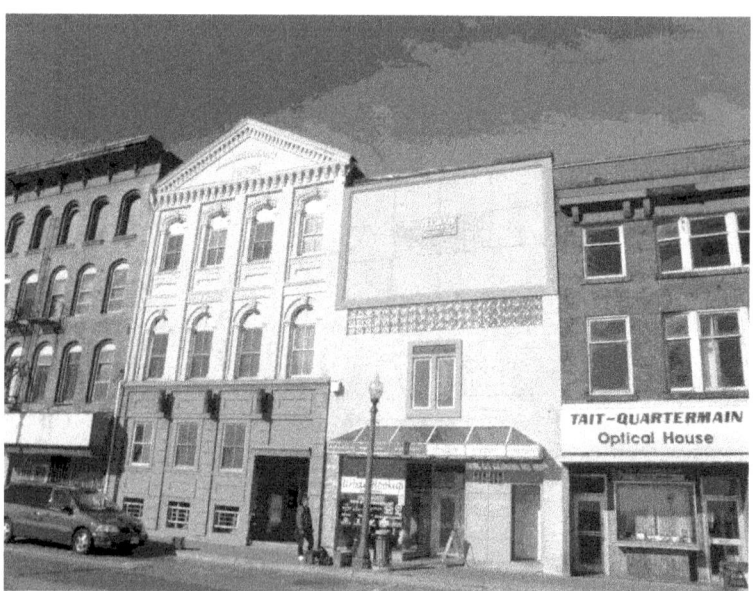

Masonic Hall 1869   Nyman Building 1897

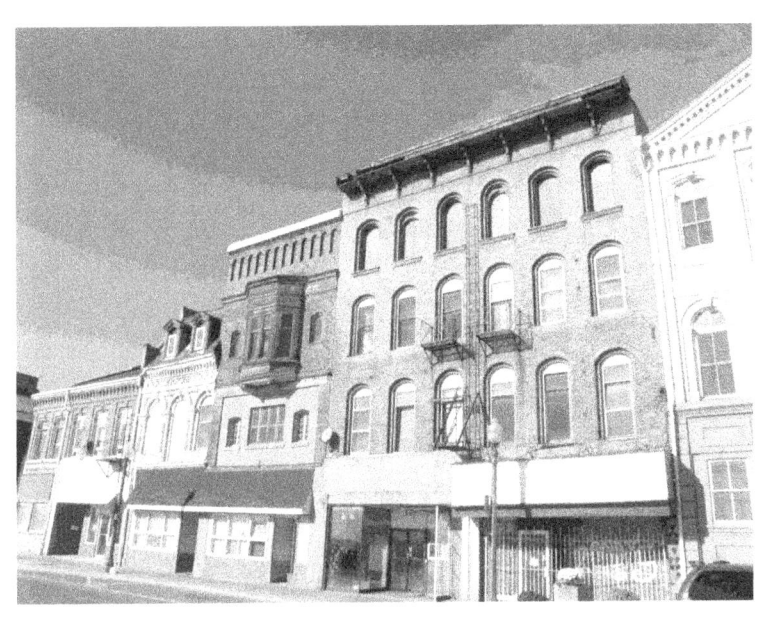

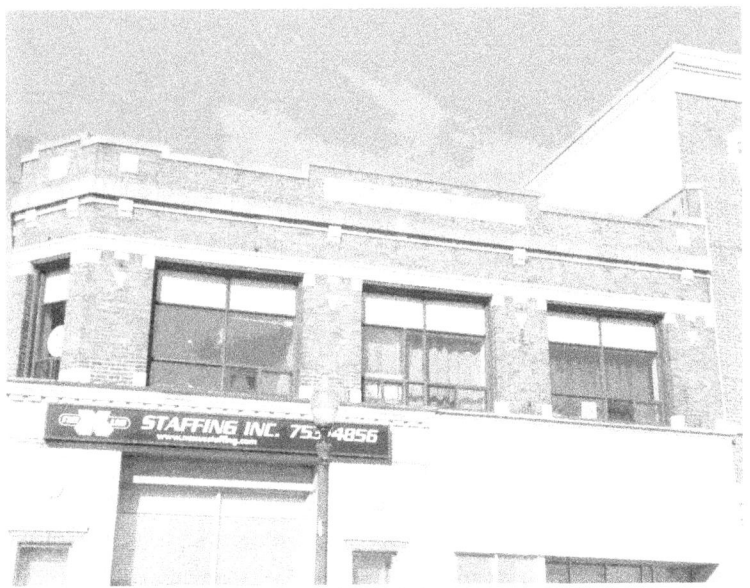

Steel Building

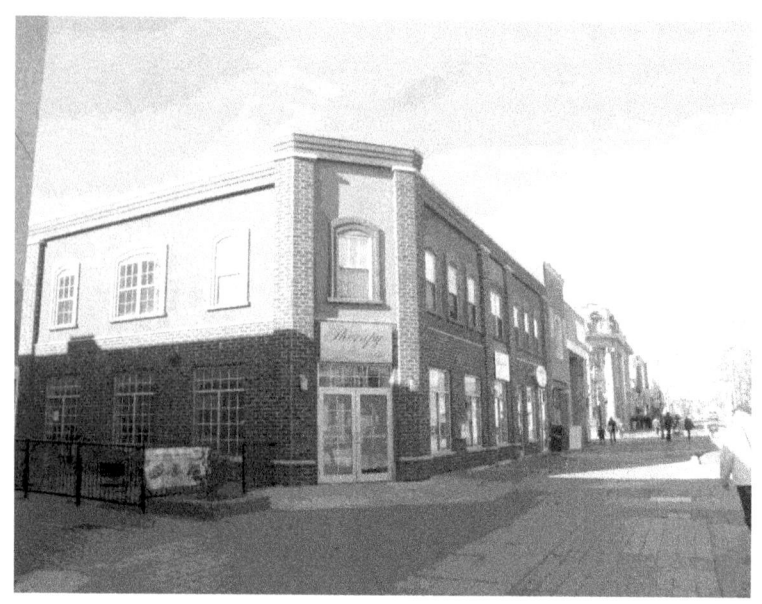

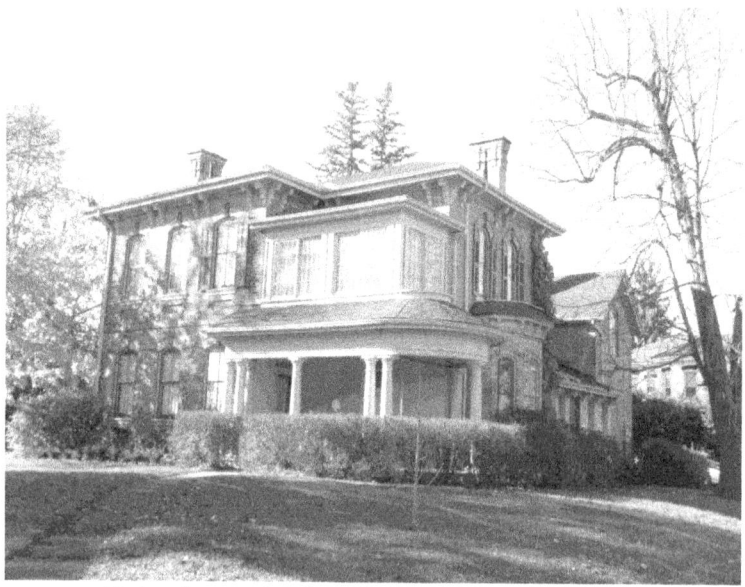

Paired cornice brackets under the eaves

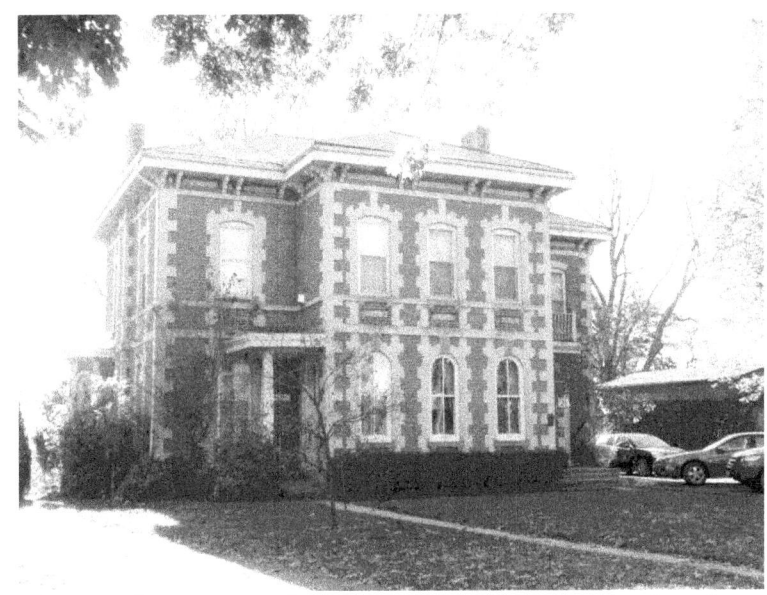

1875 with two-tone brickwork, paired cornice brackets

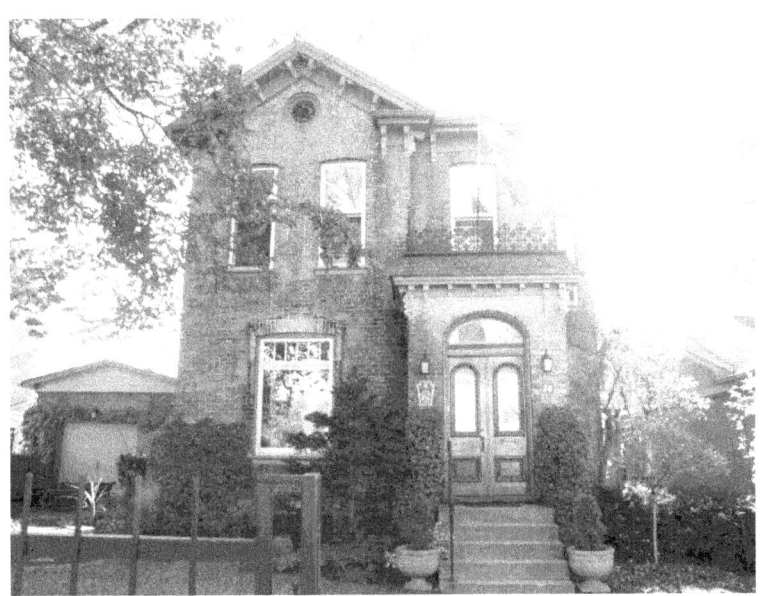

1892 – single cornice brackets, cornice return on the gable

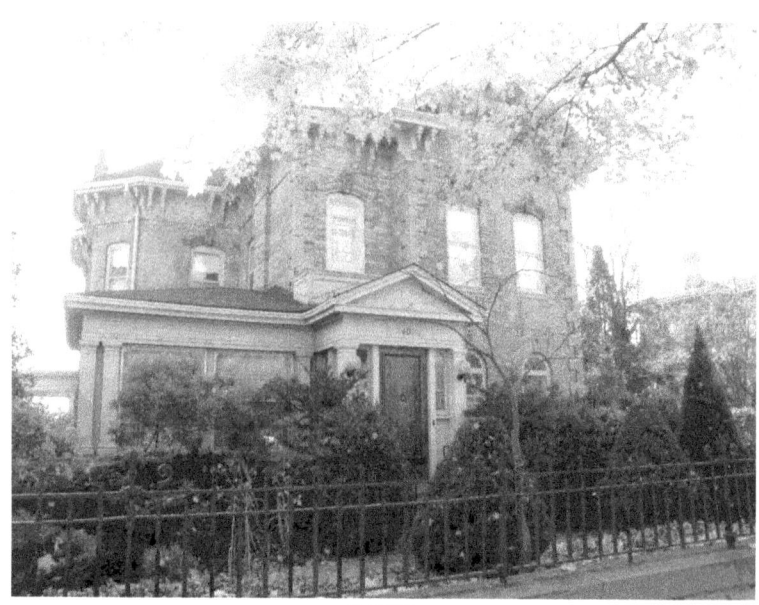

1875

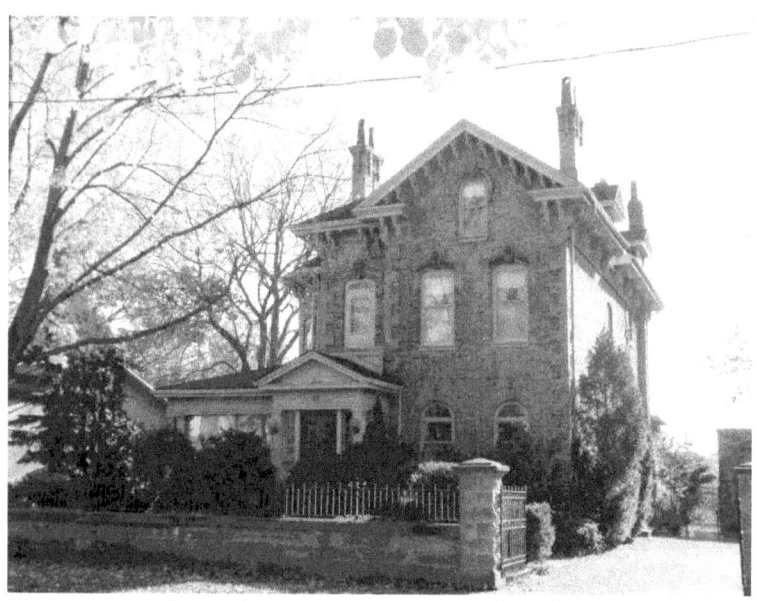

Many decorative cornice brackets

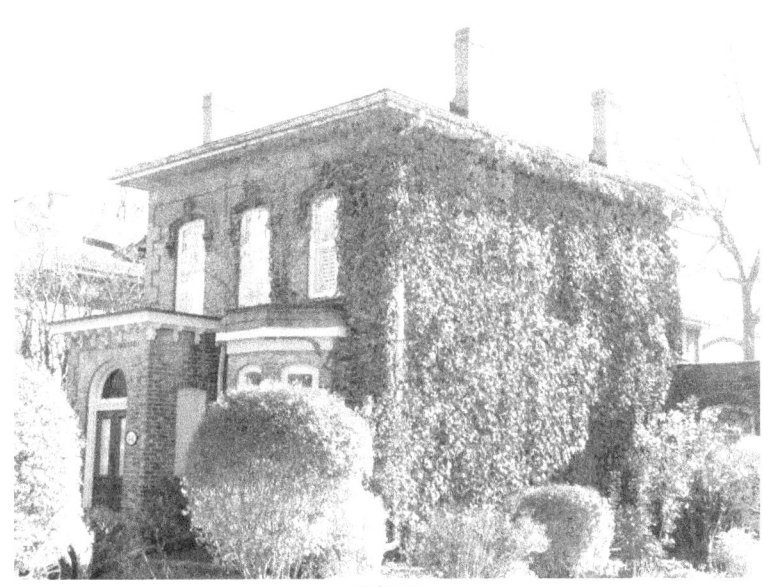

1875

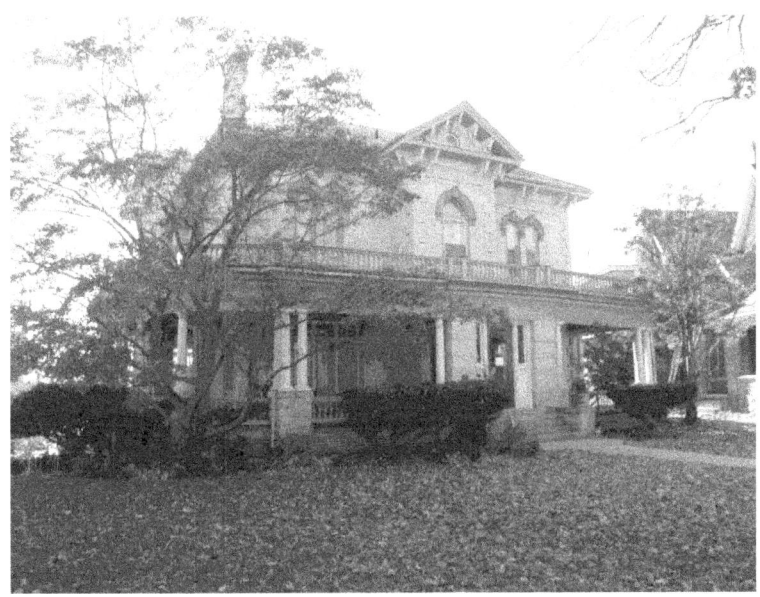

1874

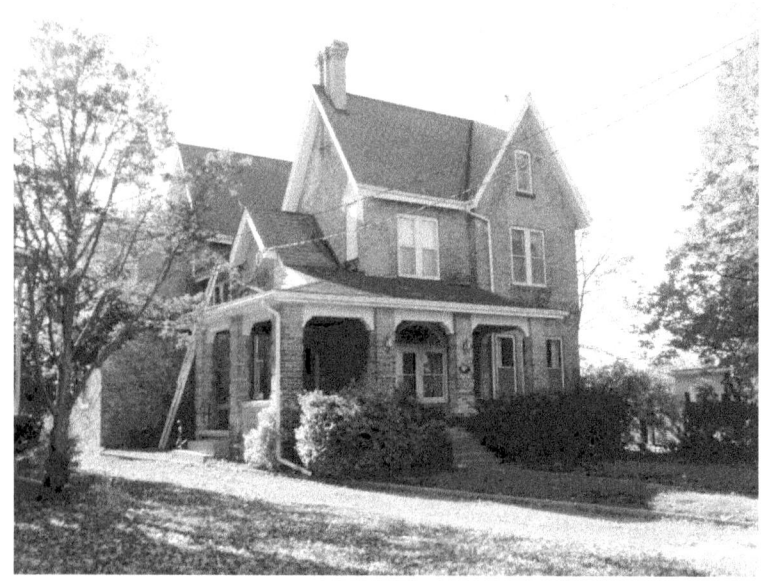

1887

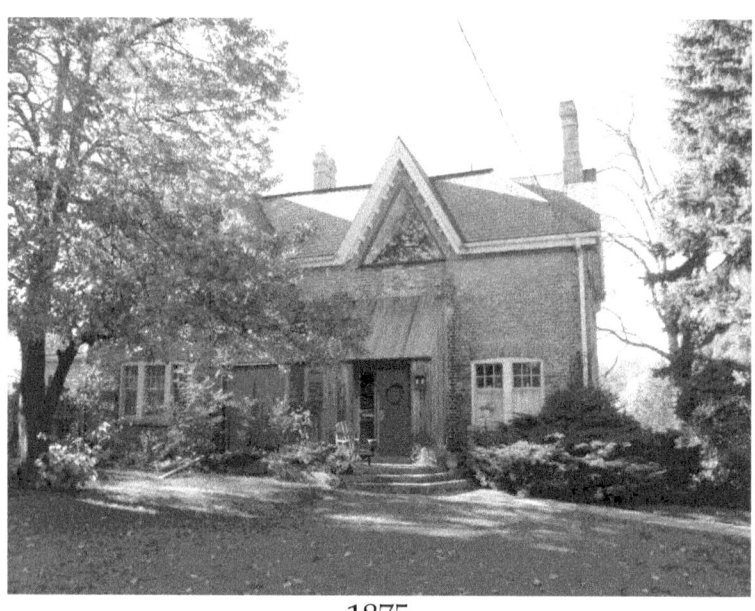

1875

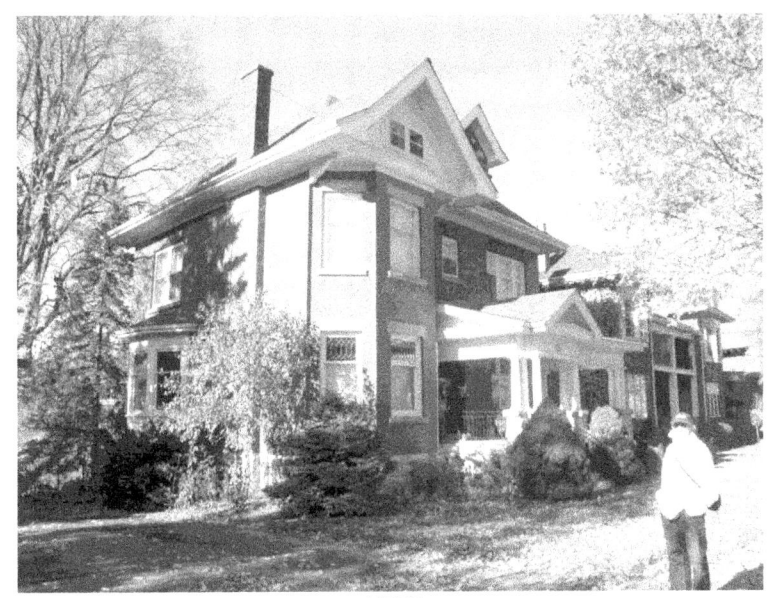

1895

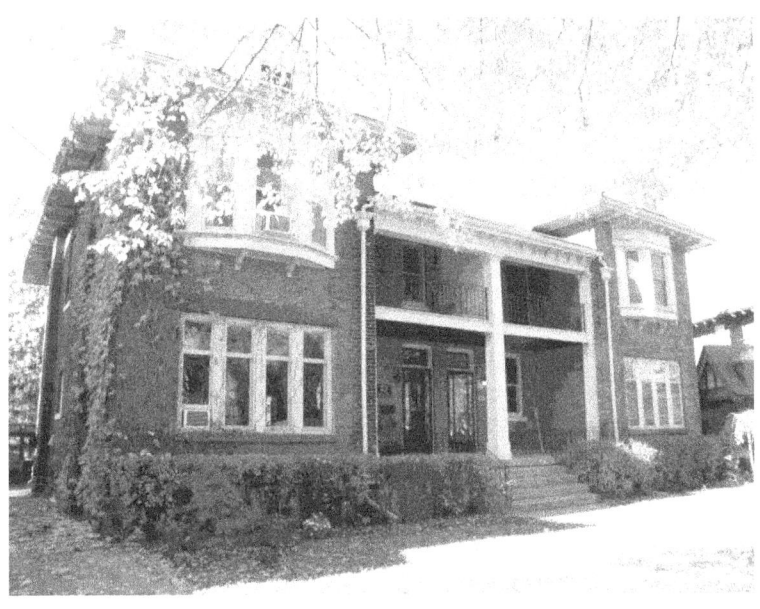

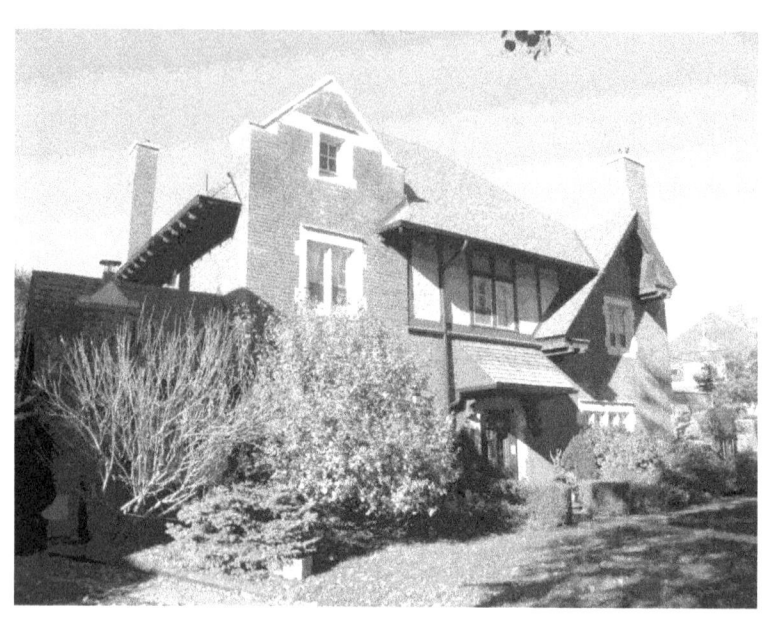

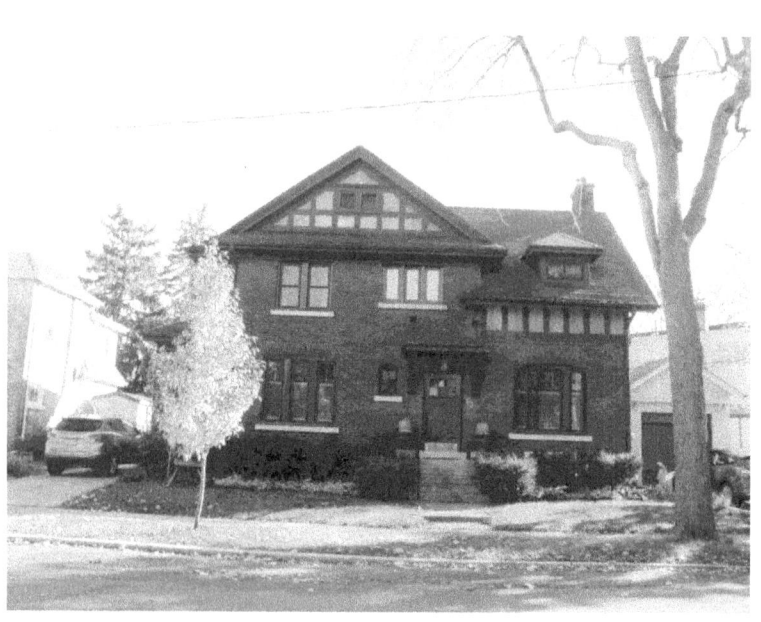

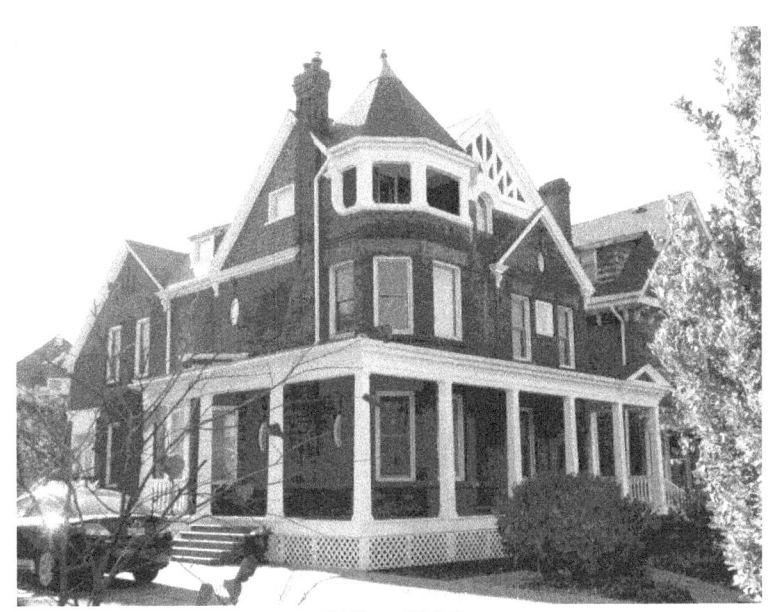

#38 – 1898

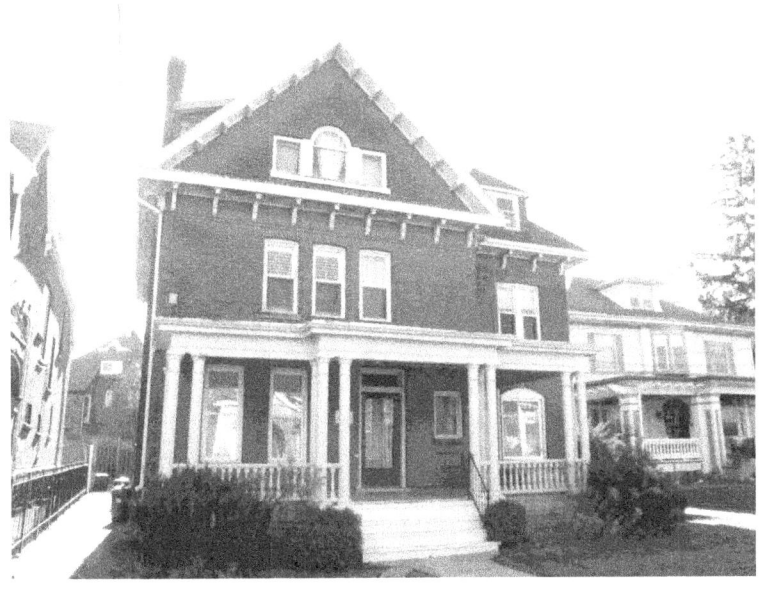

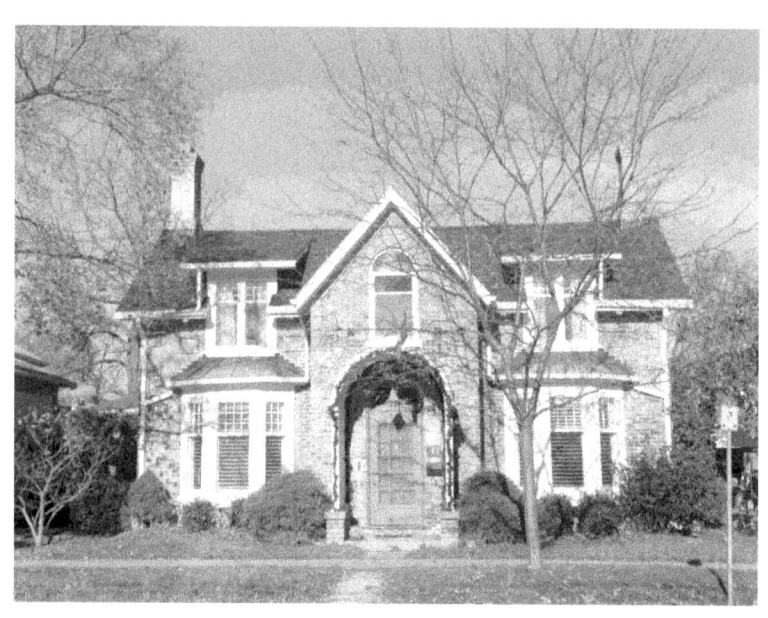

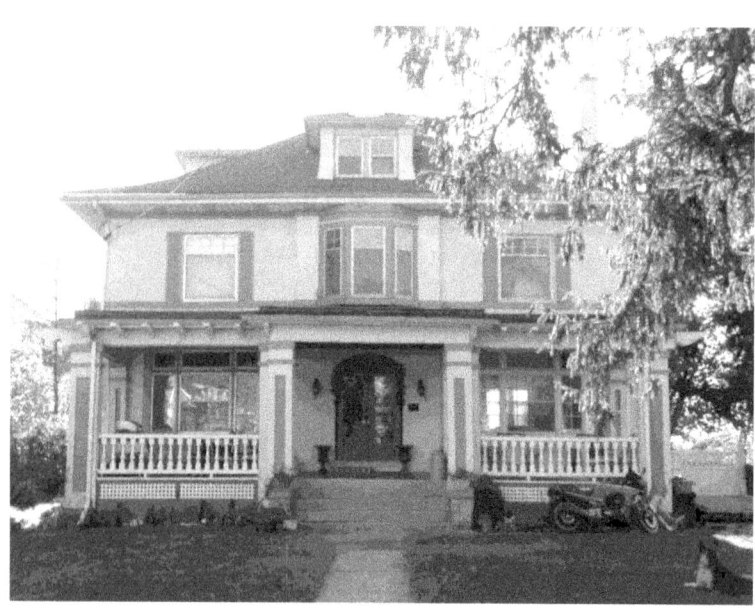

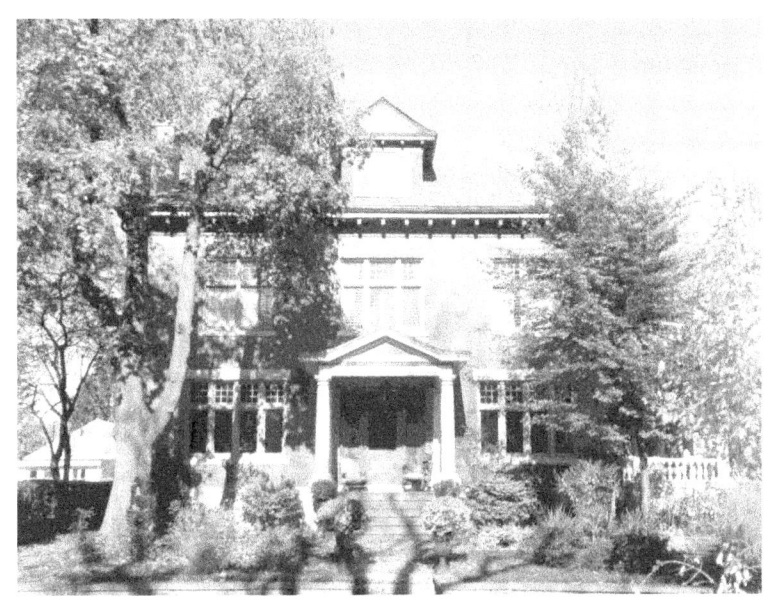

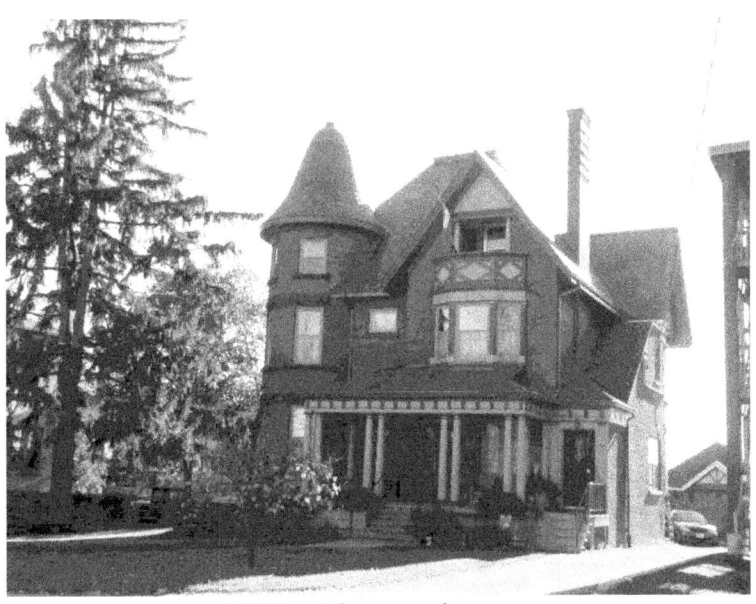

1896 with round turret

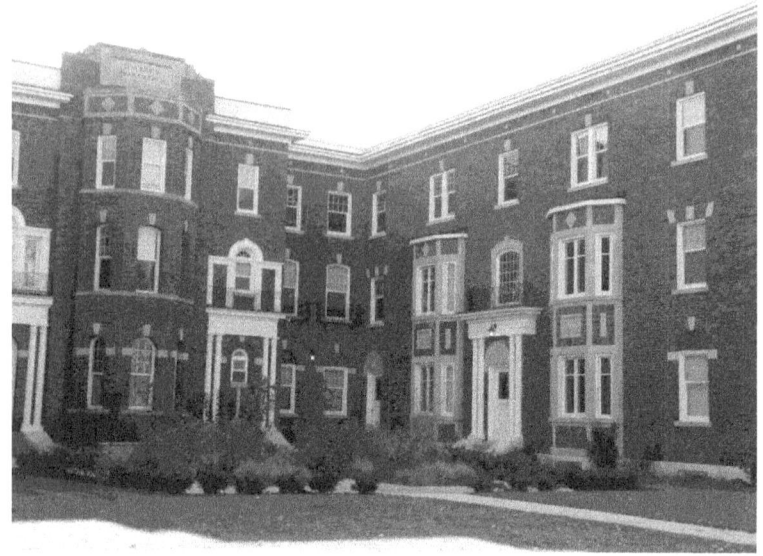

54 Dufferin Avenue

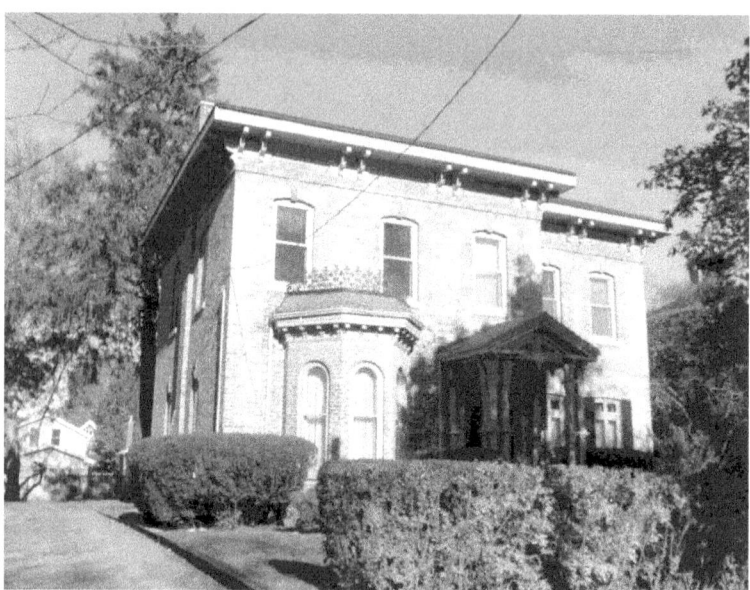

Iron cresting above bay window, paired cornice brackets

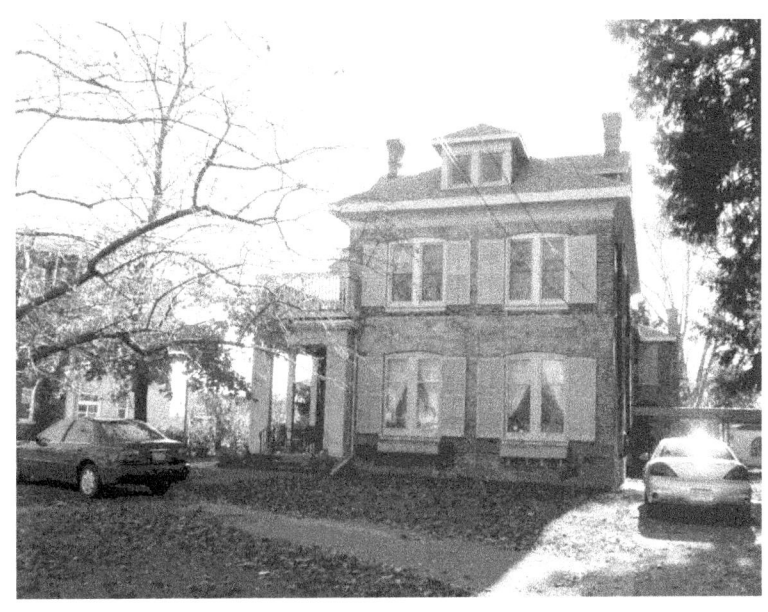

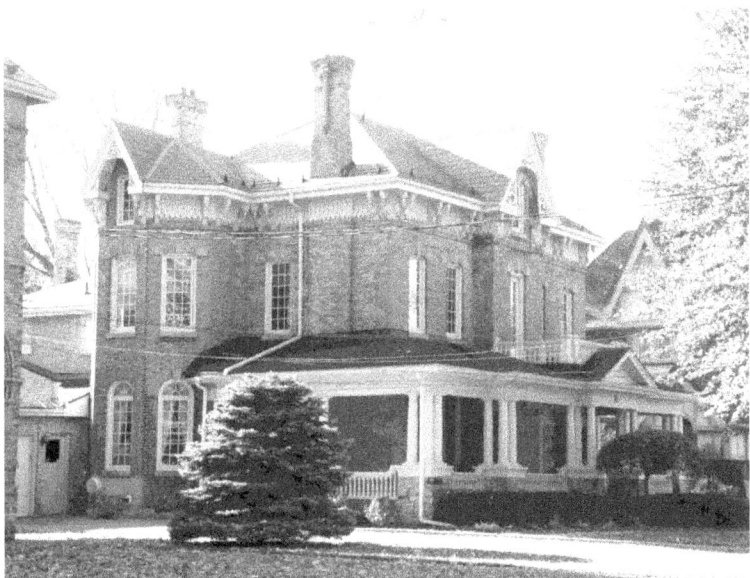

Paired cornice brackets and fancy gingerbread trim on gables

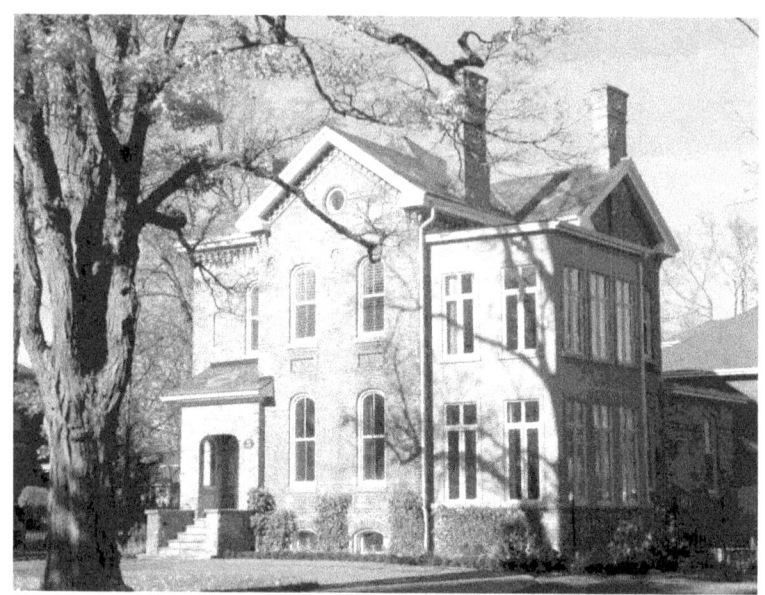
Cornice return and dentil detailing

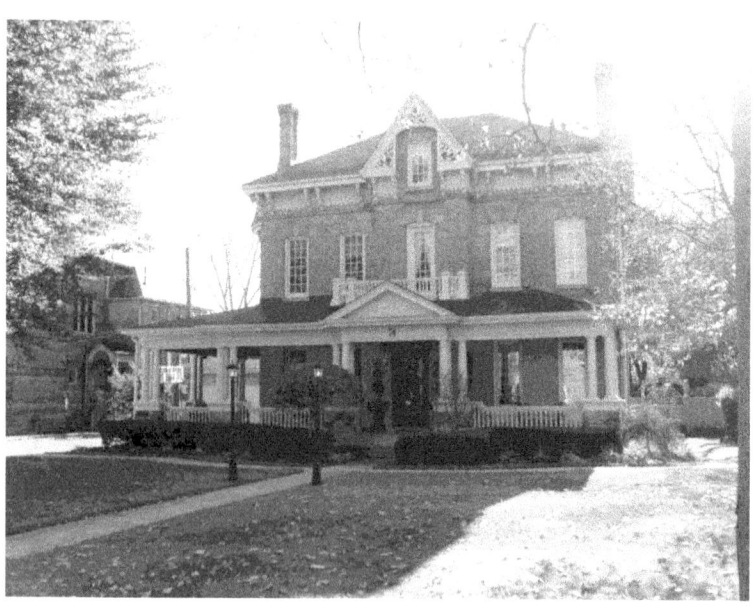

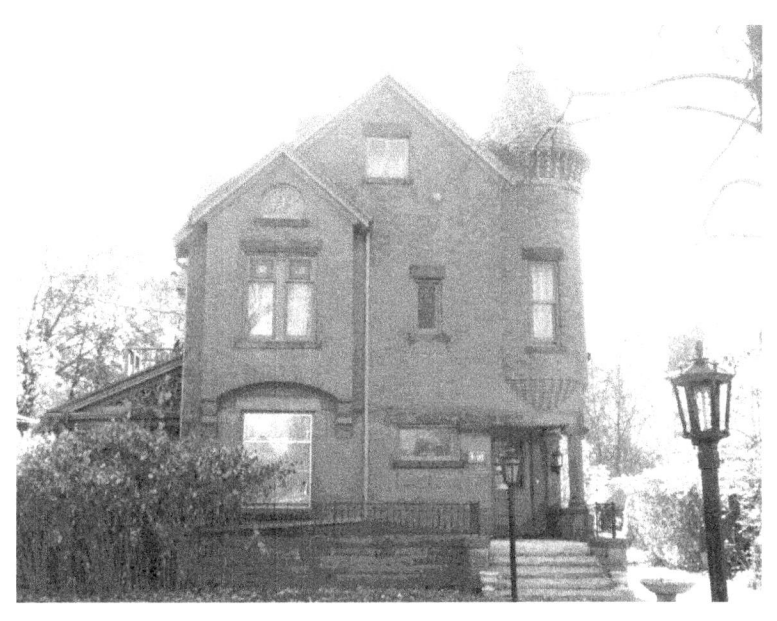

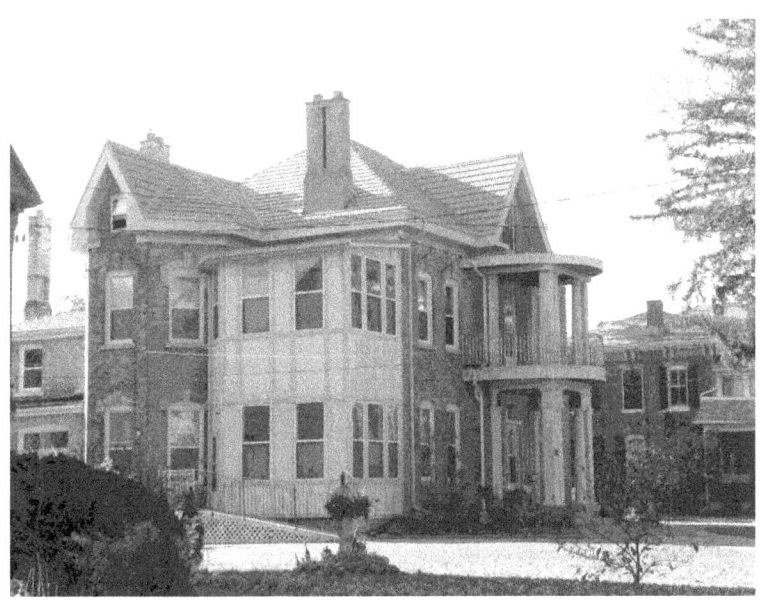

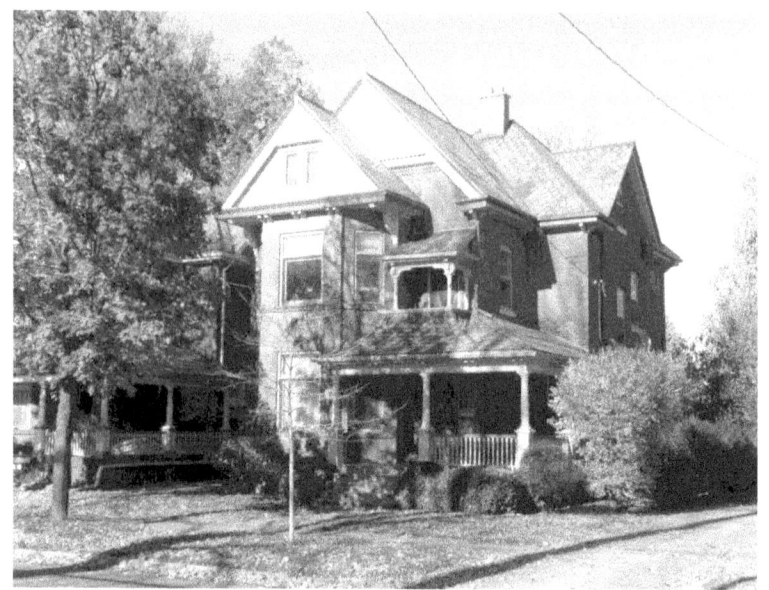

1899 – patterned roof

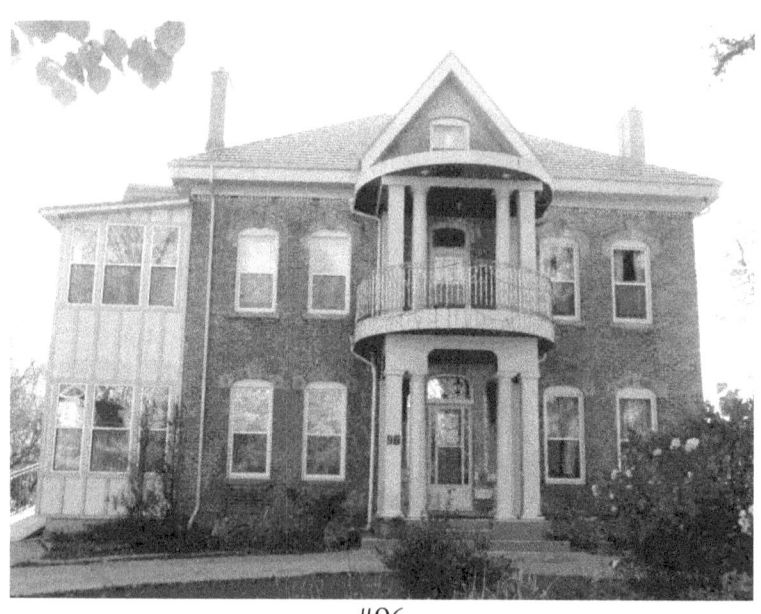

#96

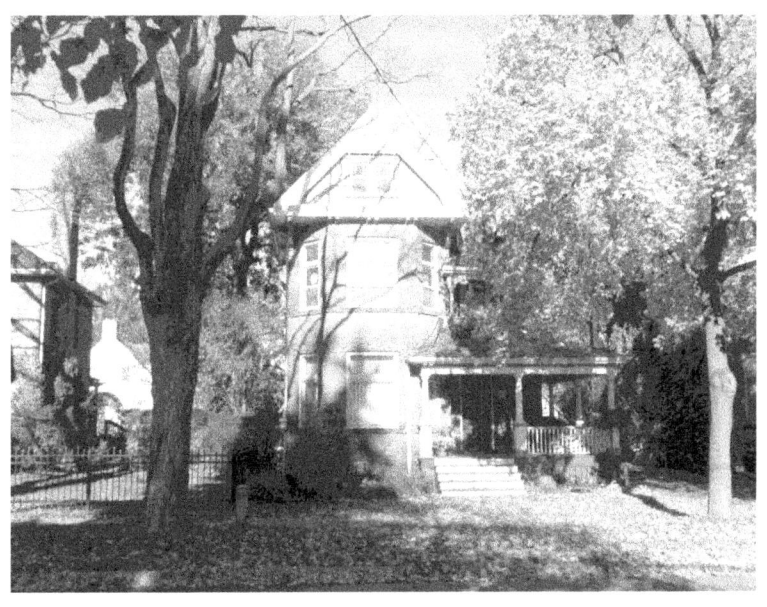

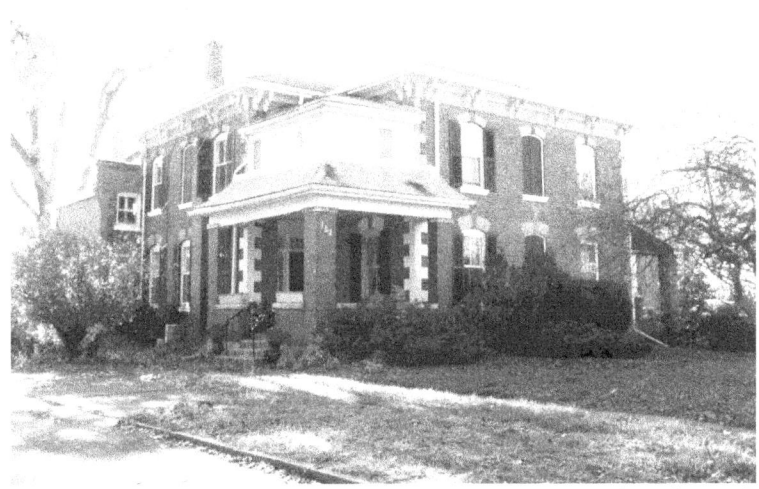

#102 with paired cornice brackets, two-tone brickwork

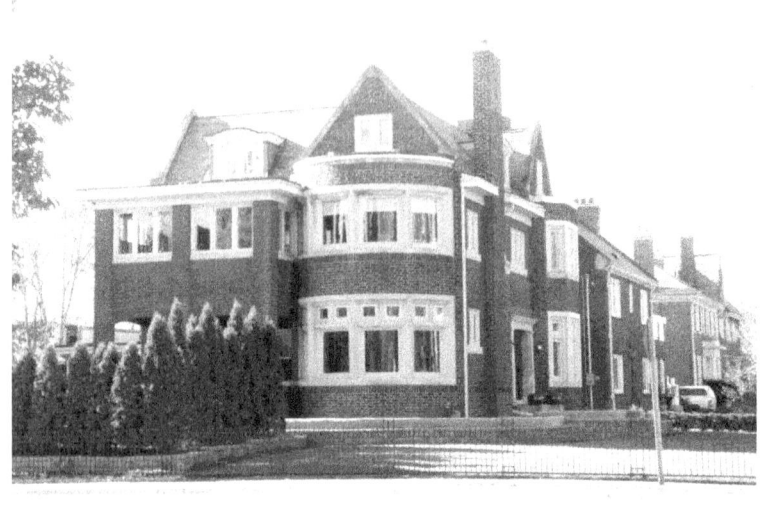

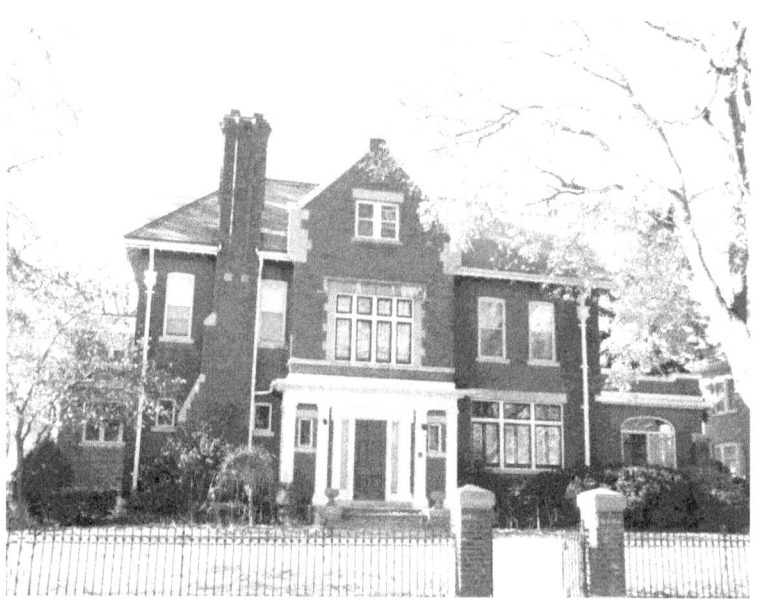

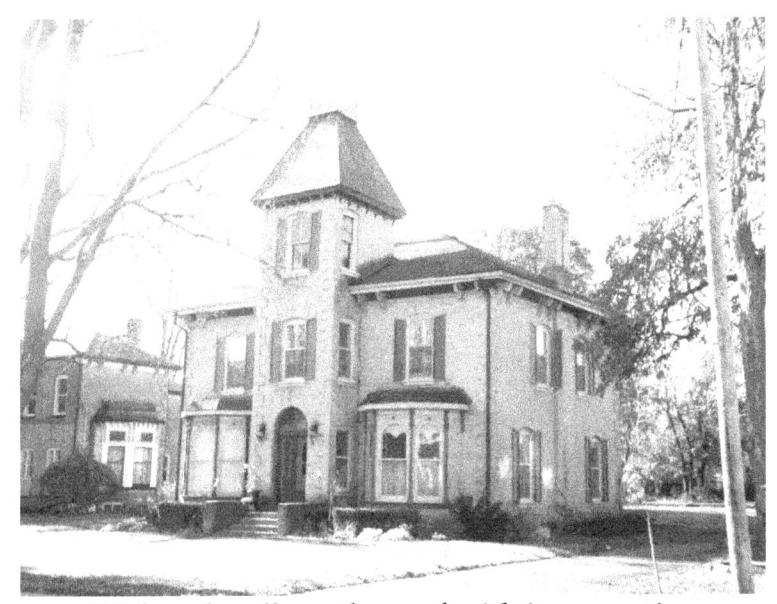

Widows' walk on the roof with iron cresting

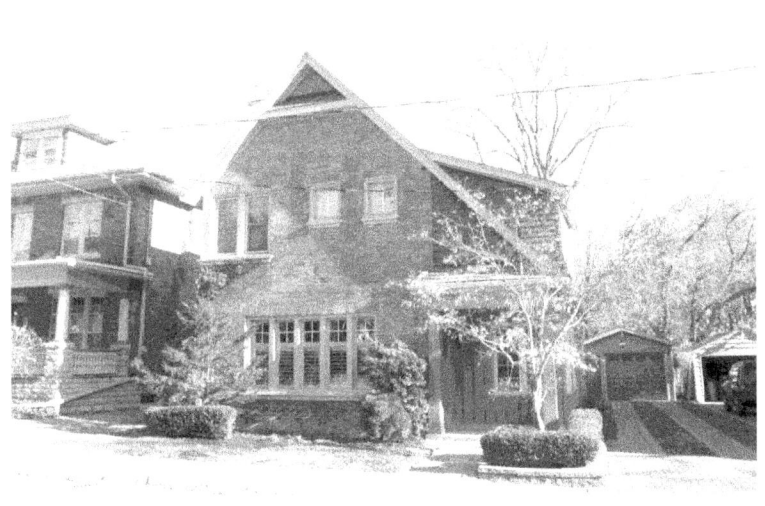

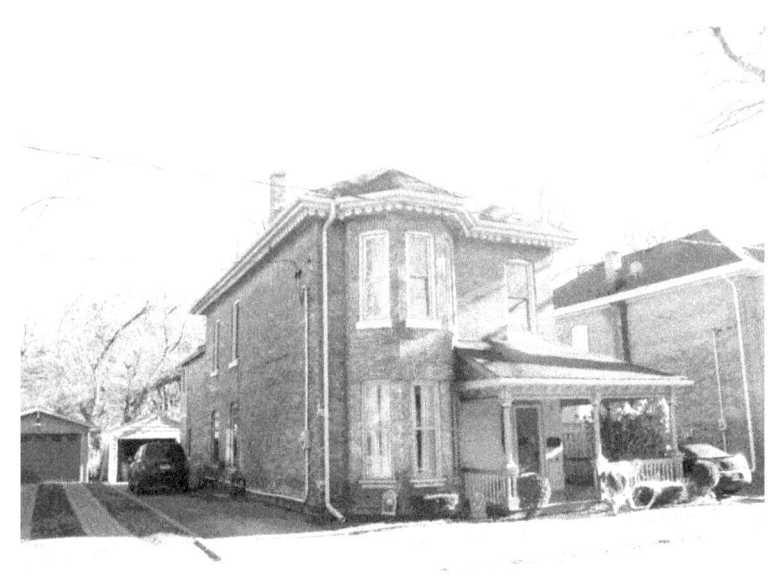

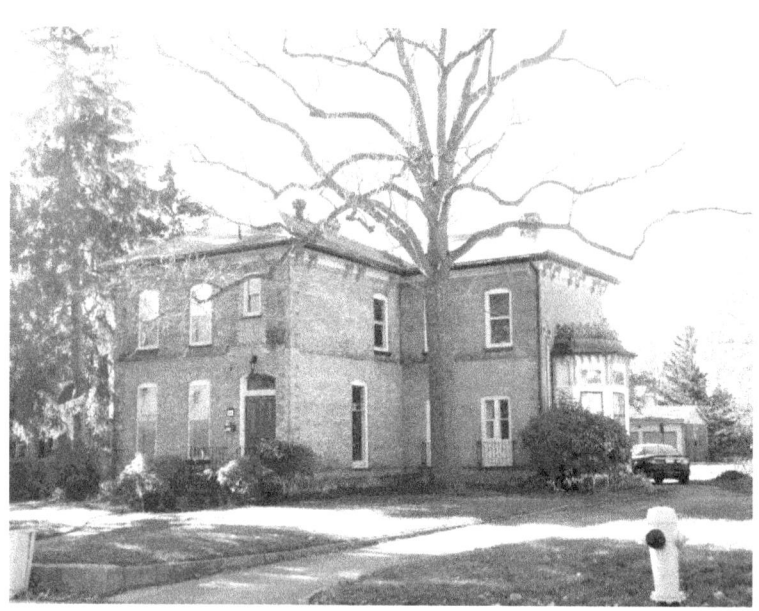

#59

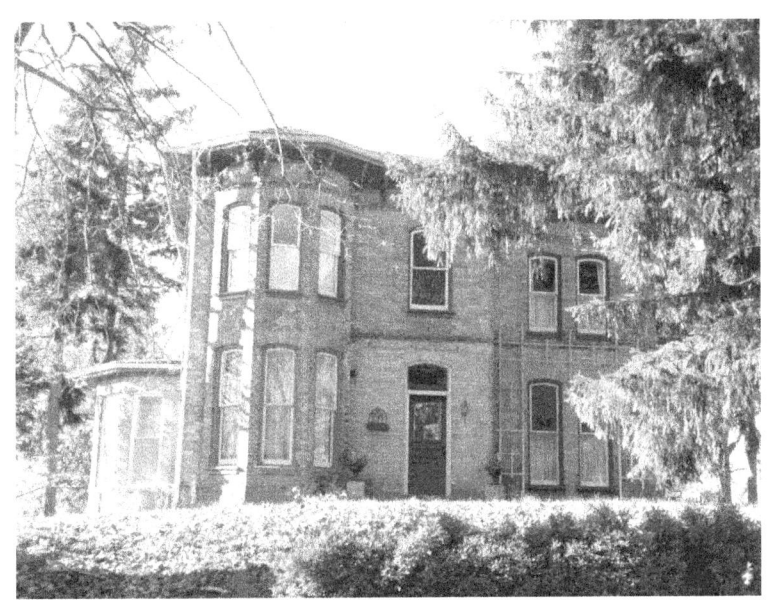

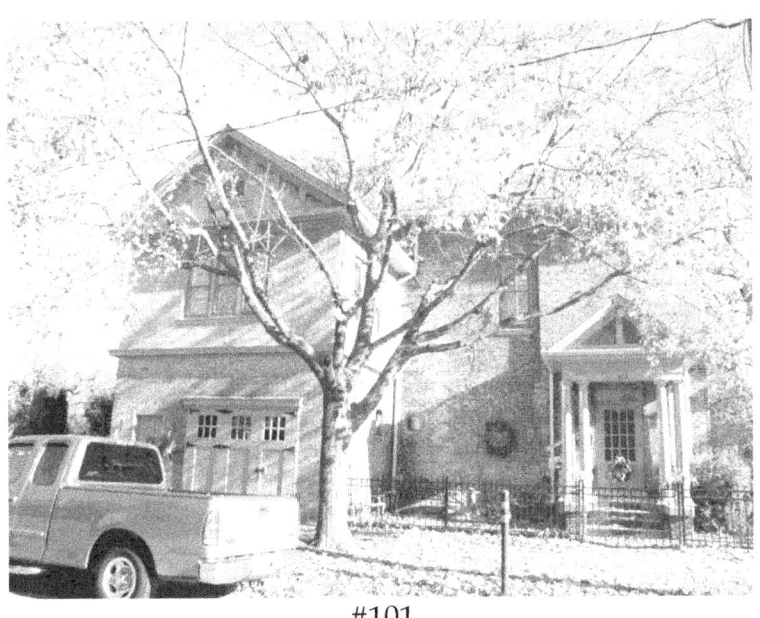

#101

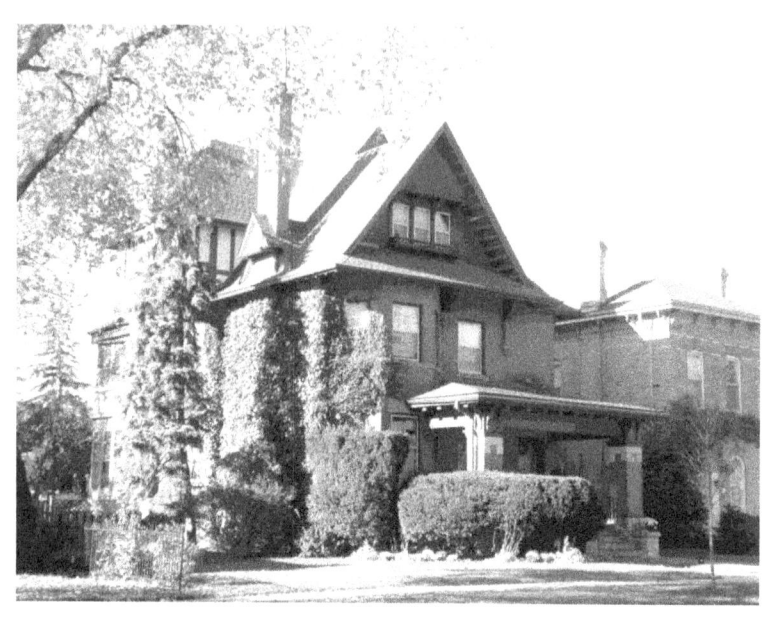

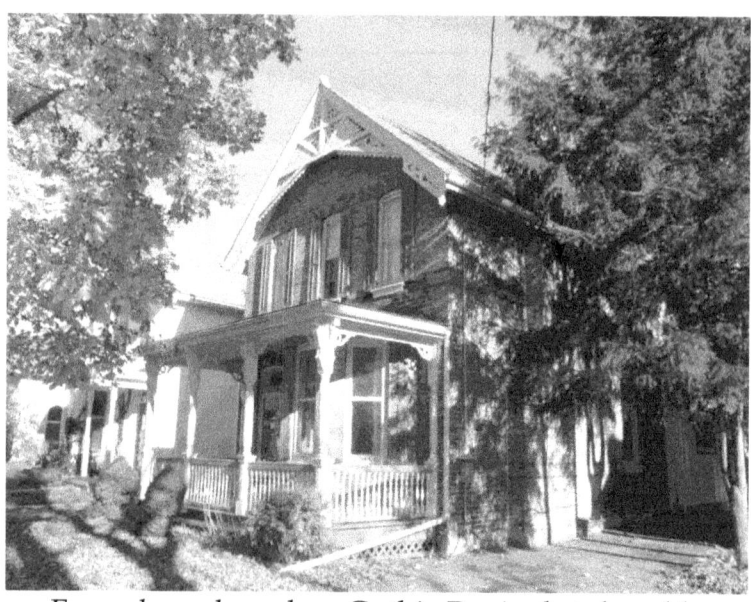

Fancy bargeboard on Gothic Revival style gable

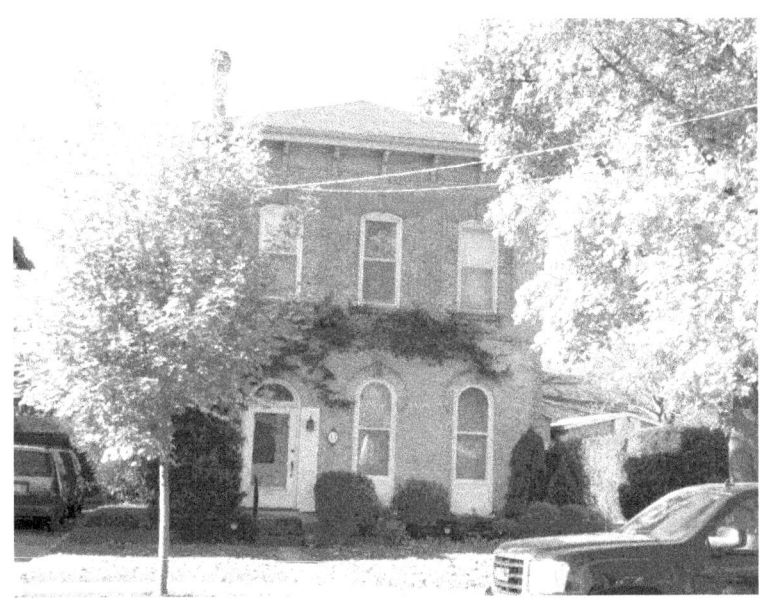

#15 – single cornice brackets under the eaves

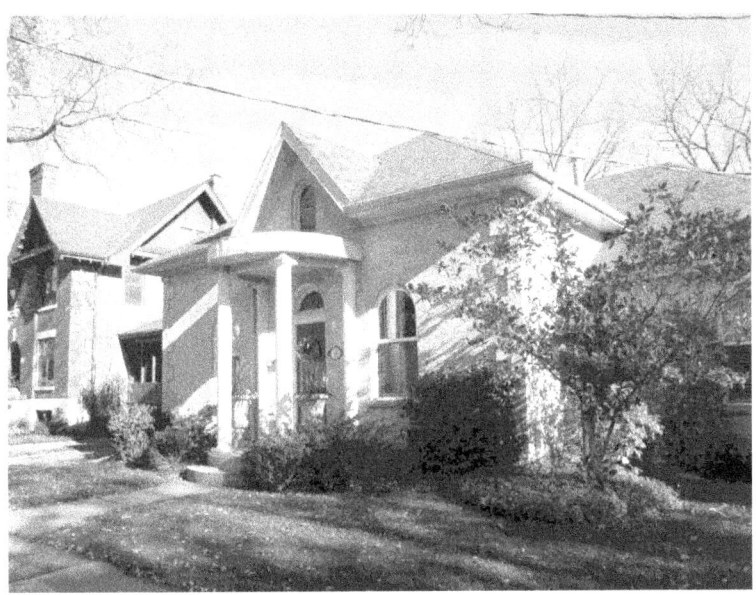

14 Chestnut Avenue

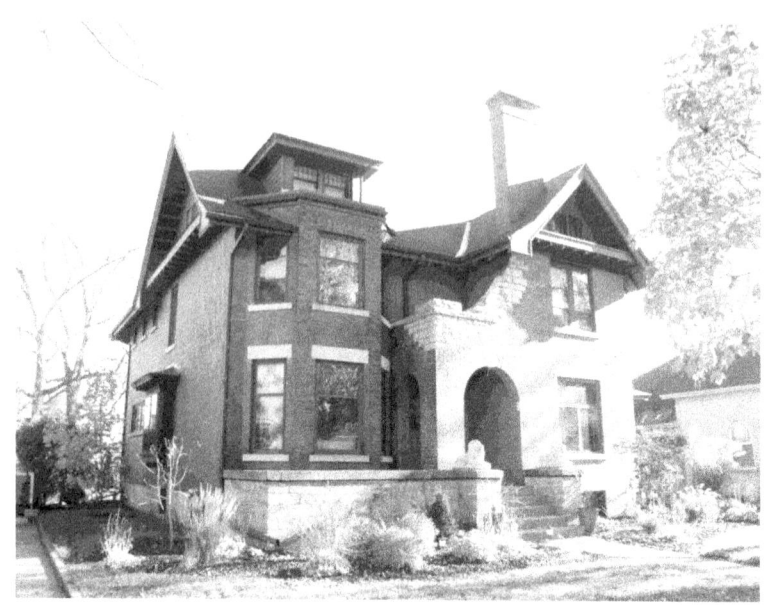

12 Chestnut Avenue

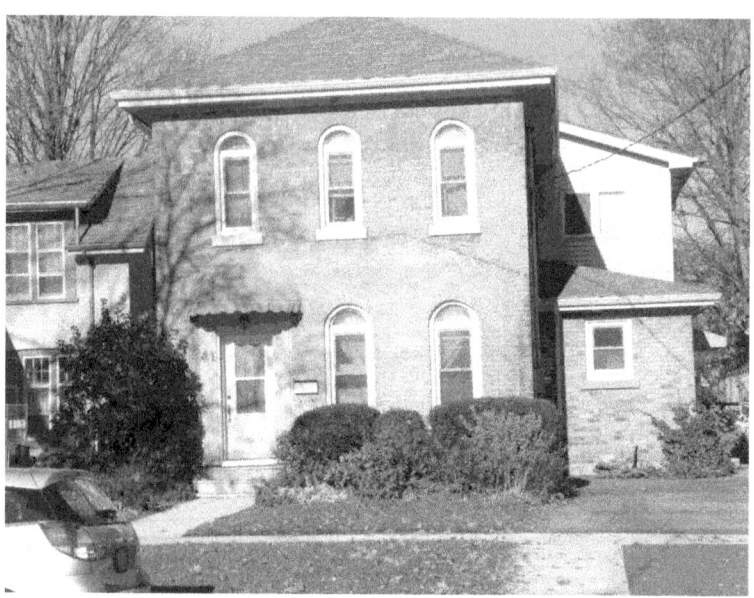

41 Chestnut Avenue

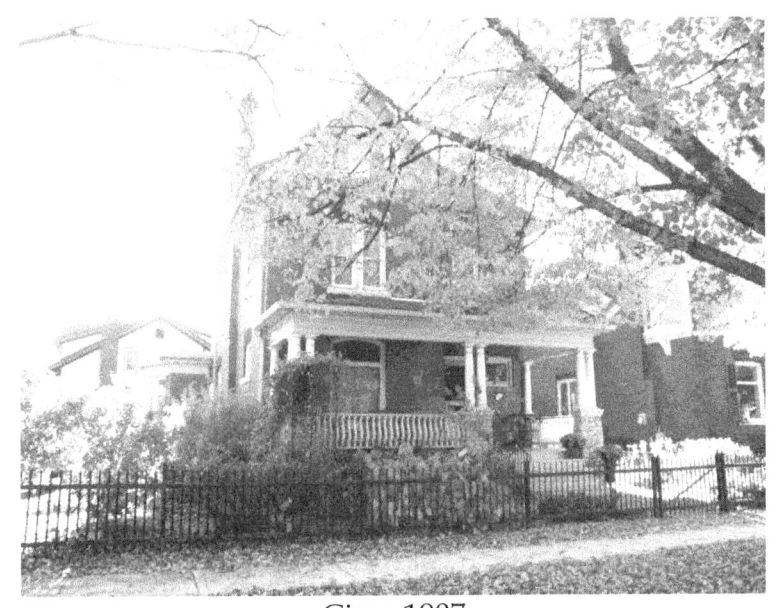

Circa 1907

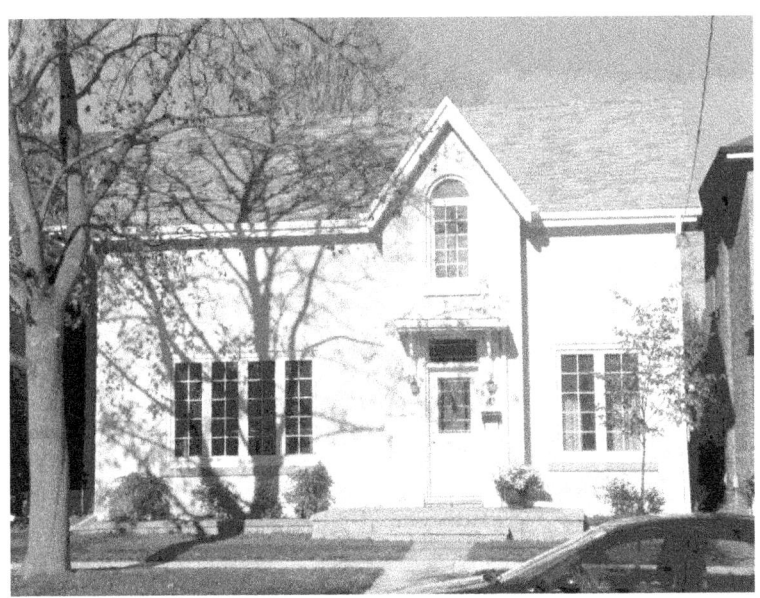

#33

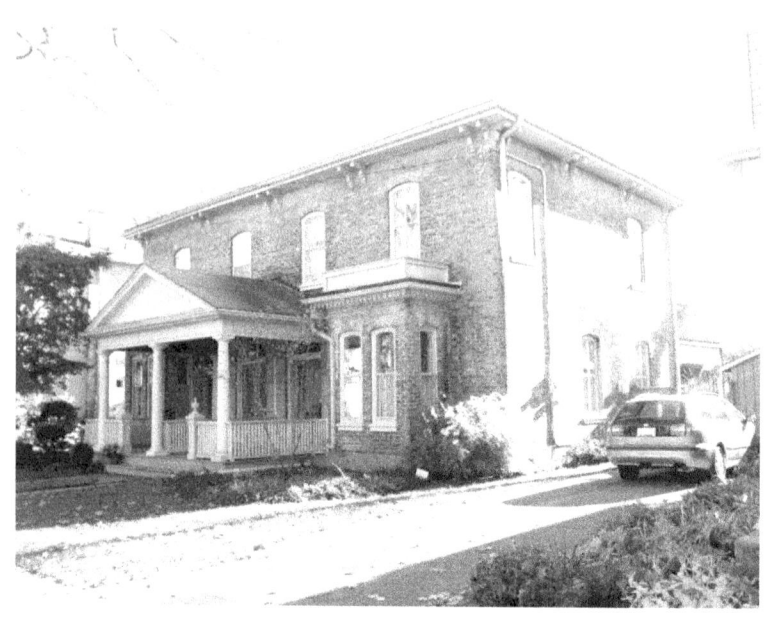

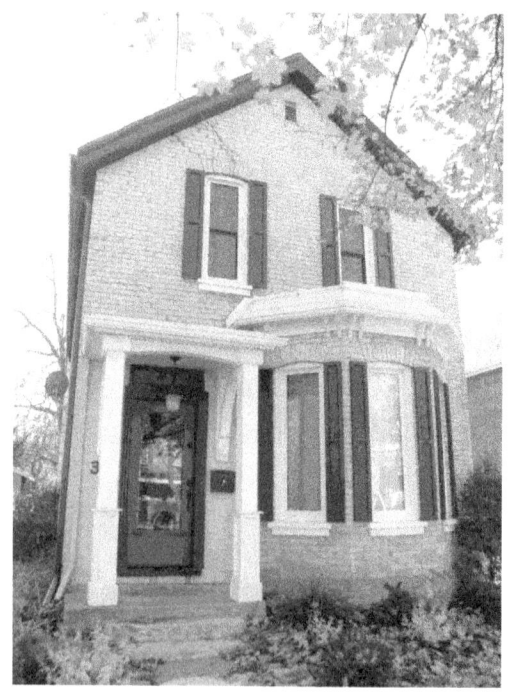

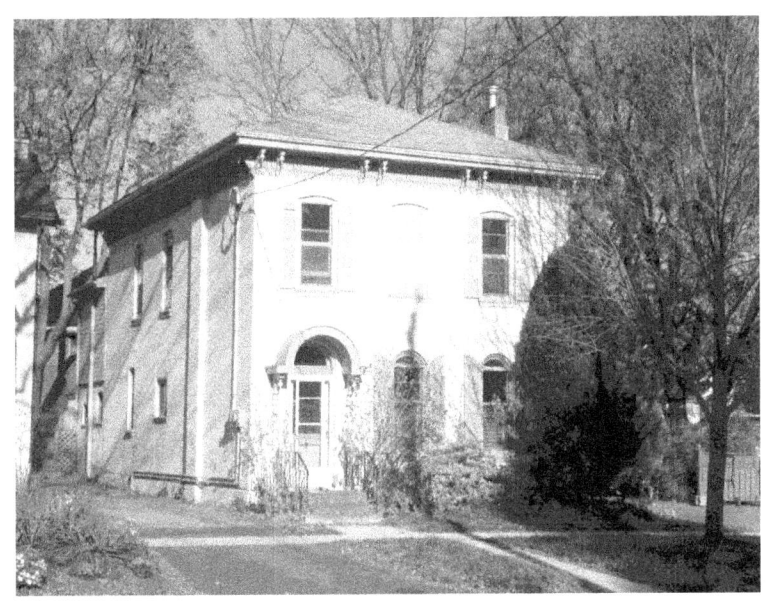

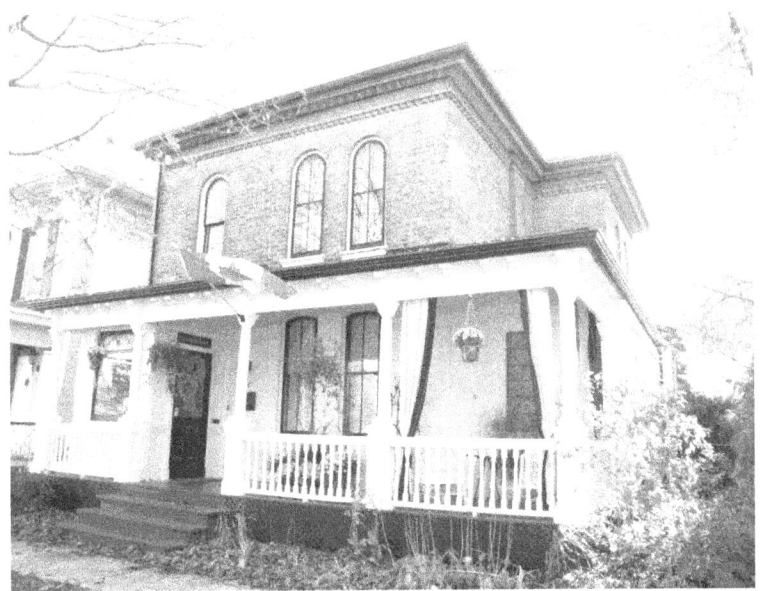

Dentil detailing in the brickwork above the upper windows

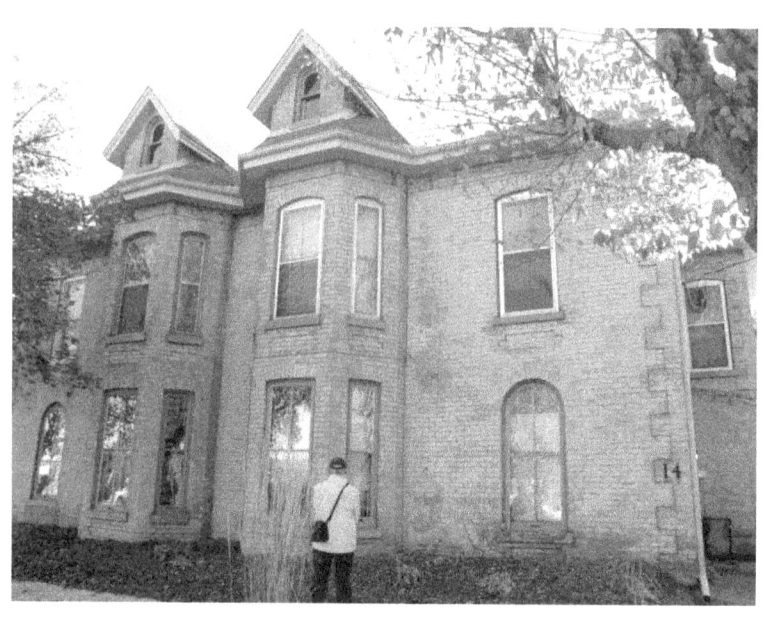

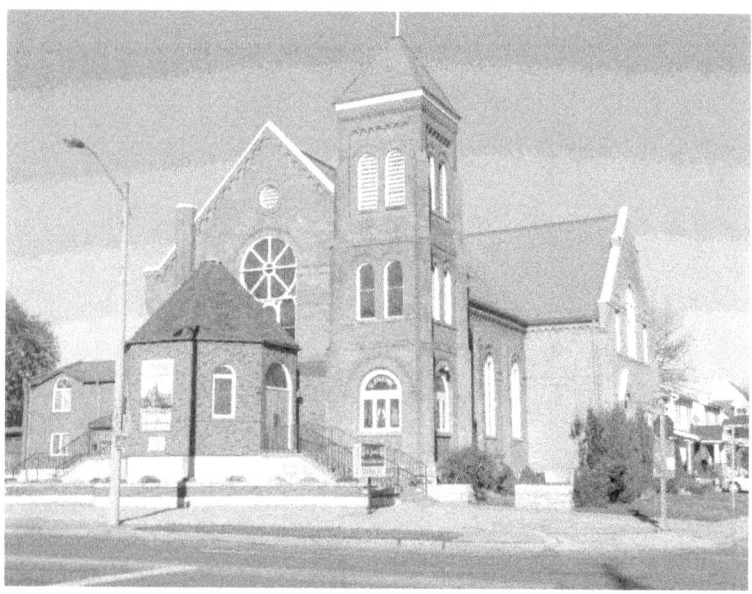

St. Joseph Roman Catholic Church, 235 Brant Avenue
With rose window

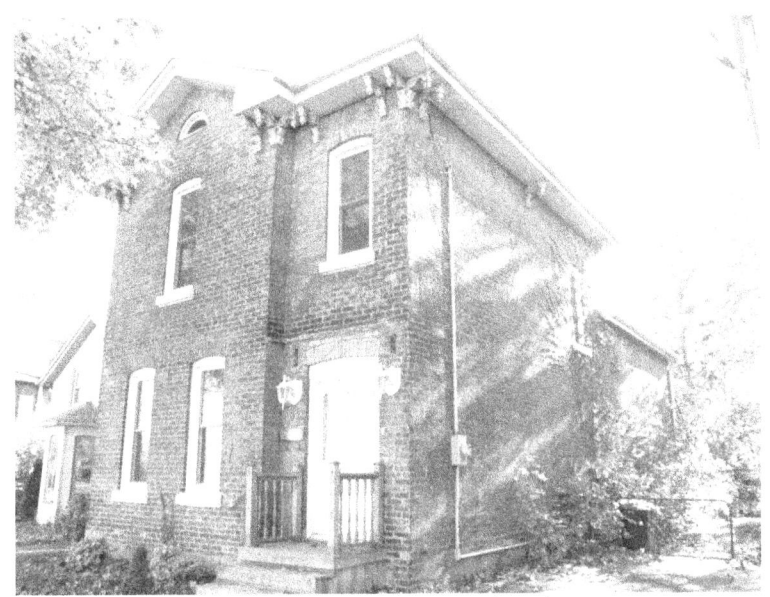

Paired cornice brackets under the eaves

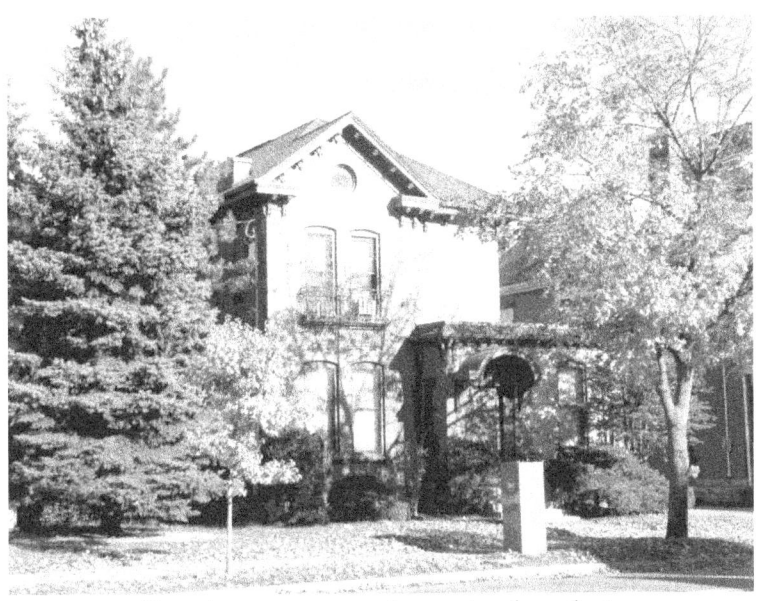

Cornice return and cornice brackets

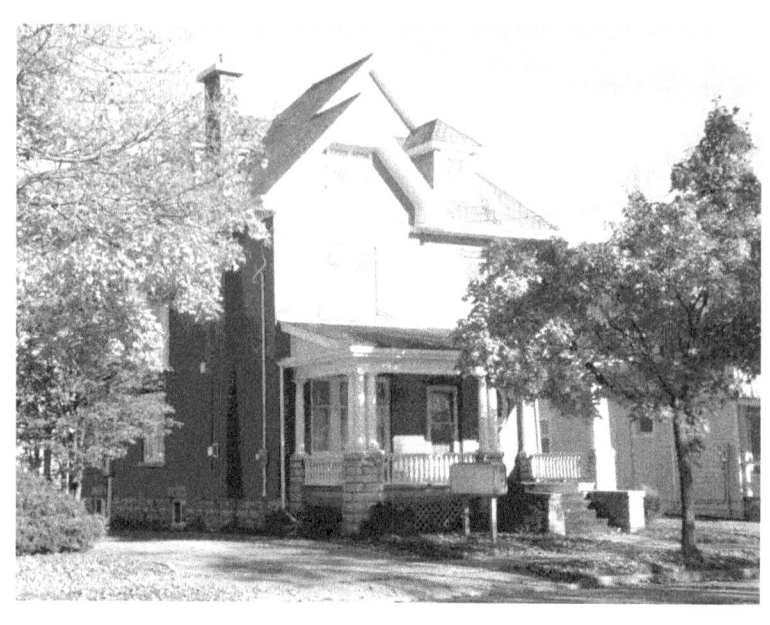

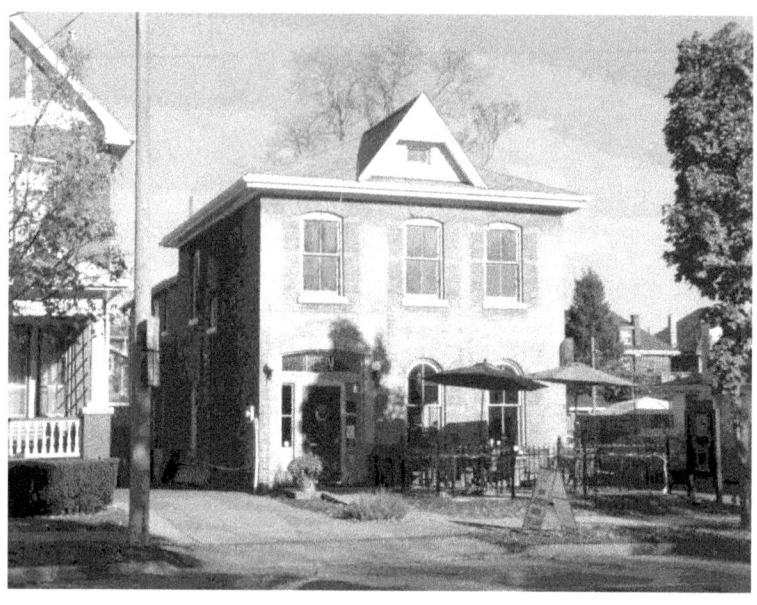

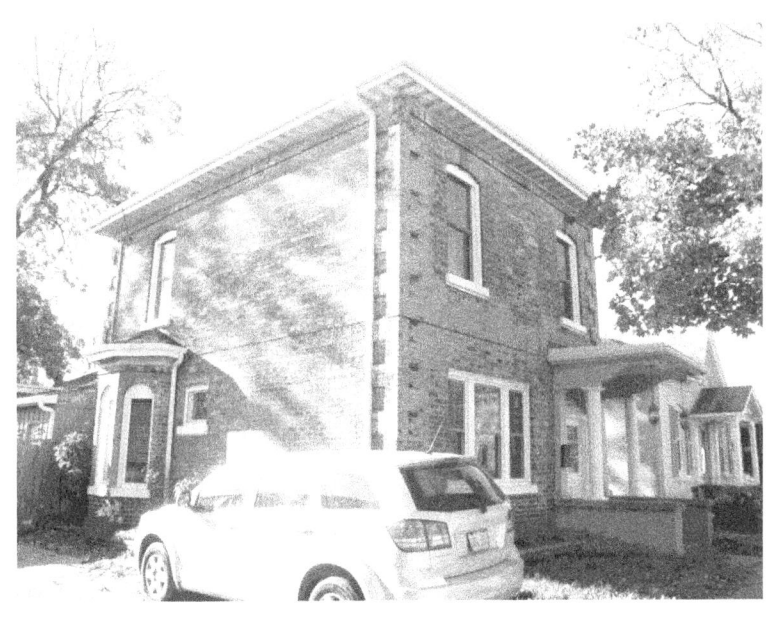

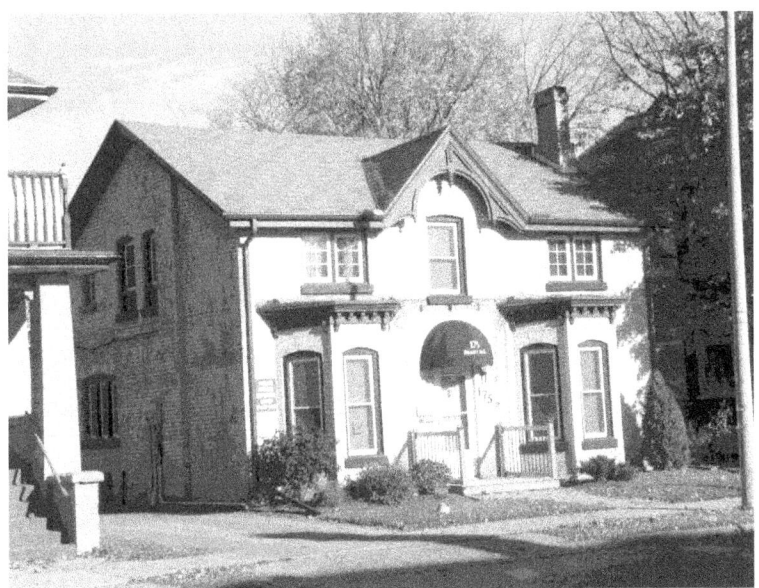

#175 with decorative vergeboard on gable

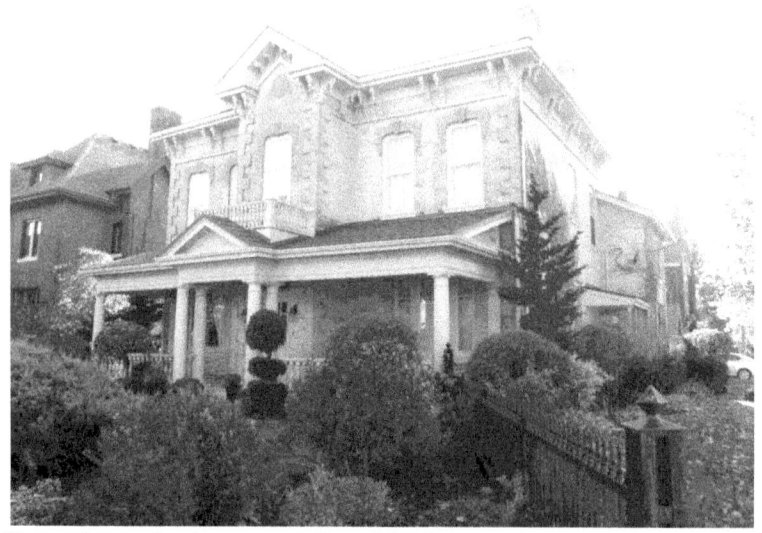

Bargeboard trim on arch with decorative cornice return
Paired cornice brackets

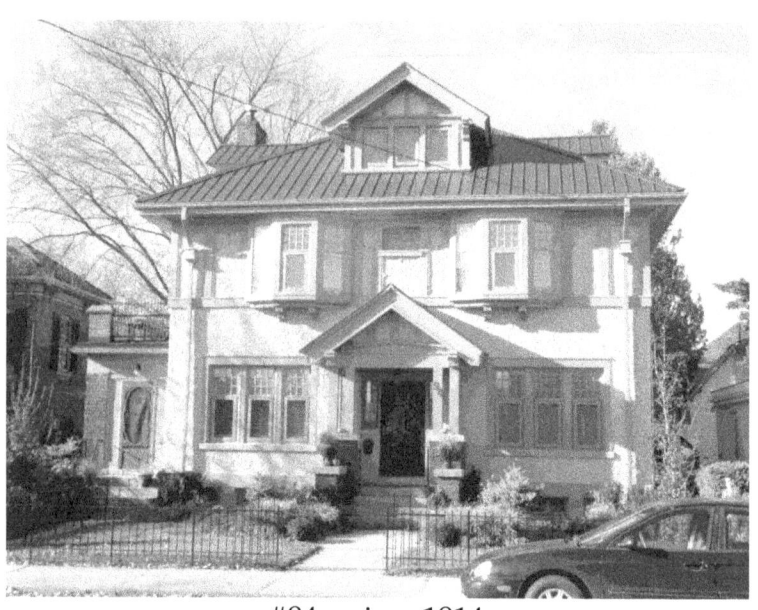

#94 – circa 1914

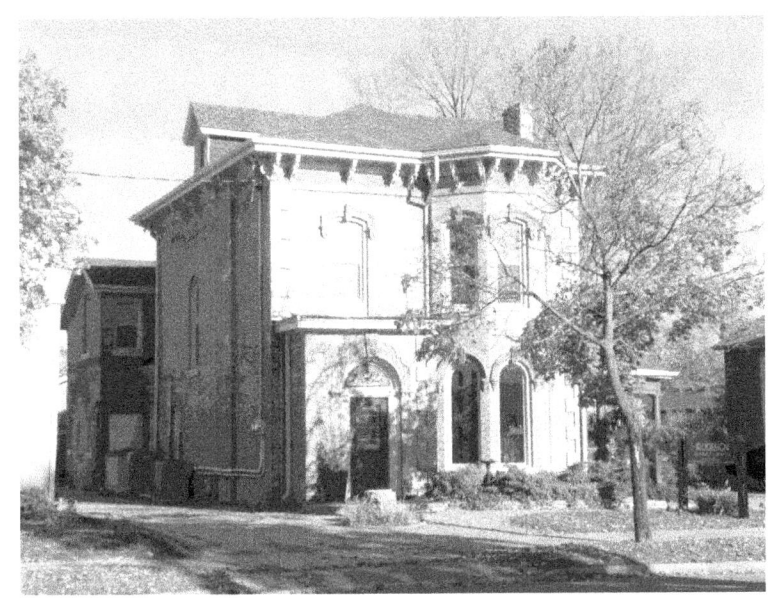

Decorative paired cornice brackets
#207

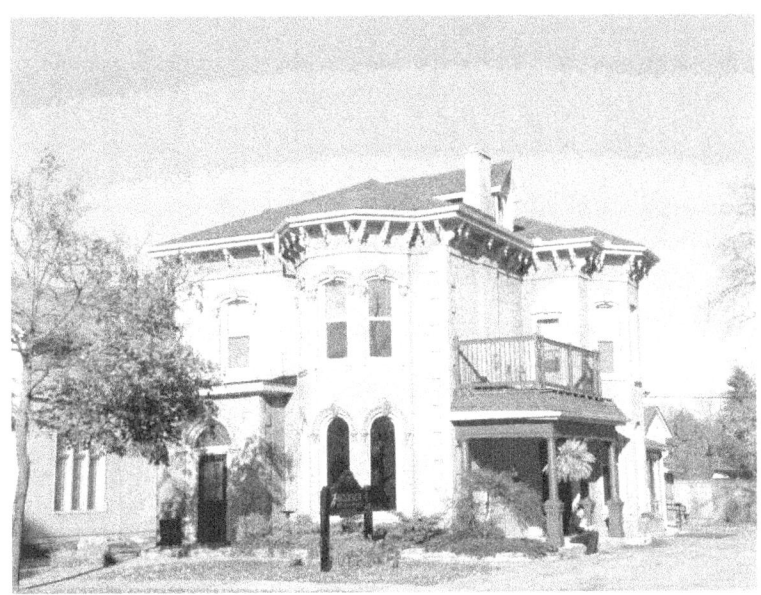

Paired cornice brackets

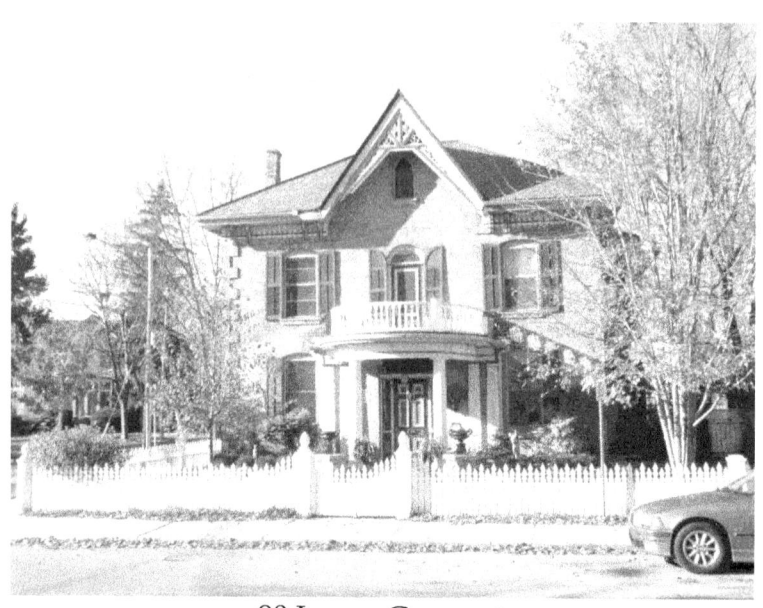

90 Lorne Crescent
Gingerbread trim on Gothic Revival style arch
Balcony on second level

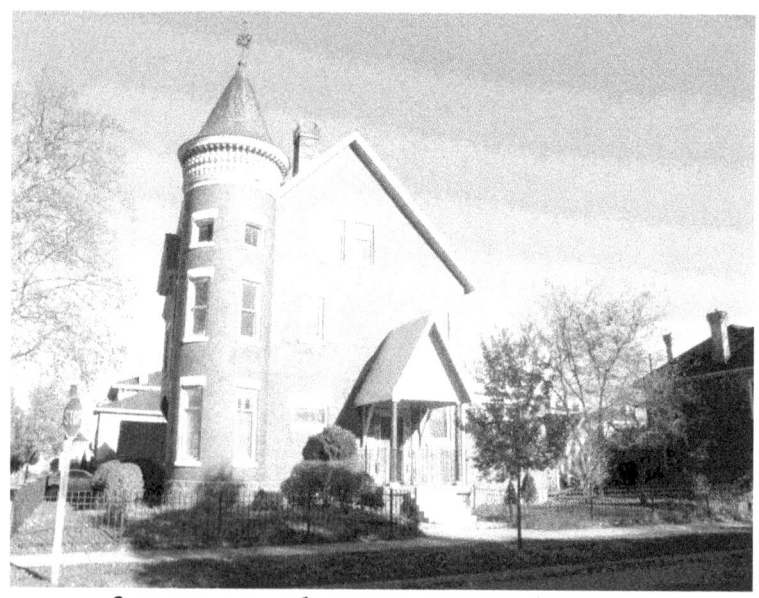

3 storey round turret room with cupola

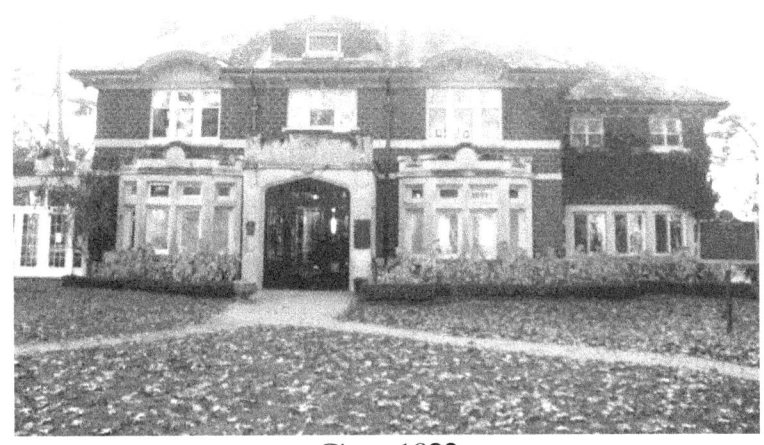

Circa 1922

Glenhyrst Art Gallery of Brantford and Glenhyrst Gardens which overlook the Grand River

Born into a prominent Brantford family, Lawren Harris (1885-1970) began to paint as a child. At the University of Toronto, a professor noticed he sketched during lectures and advised he be sent to Europe to study art. In 1920, he helped found the Group of Seven, an association of landscape artists dedicated to creating a distinctly Canadian form of art. In the 1930s, he became an abstract artist. Harris landscapes such as "North Shore, Lake Superior," and "Icebergs, Davis Strait" remain celebrated Canadian images.

Bethel Road

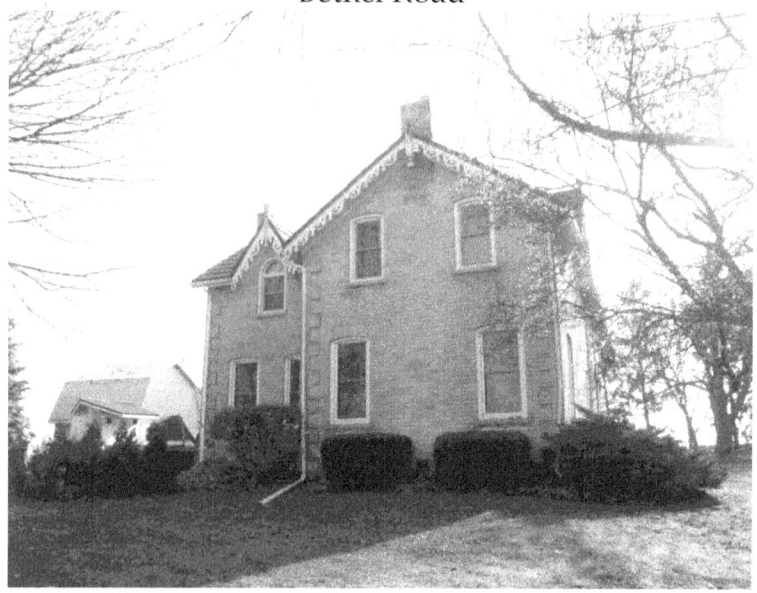

Vergeboard with finials

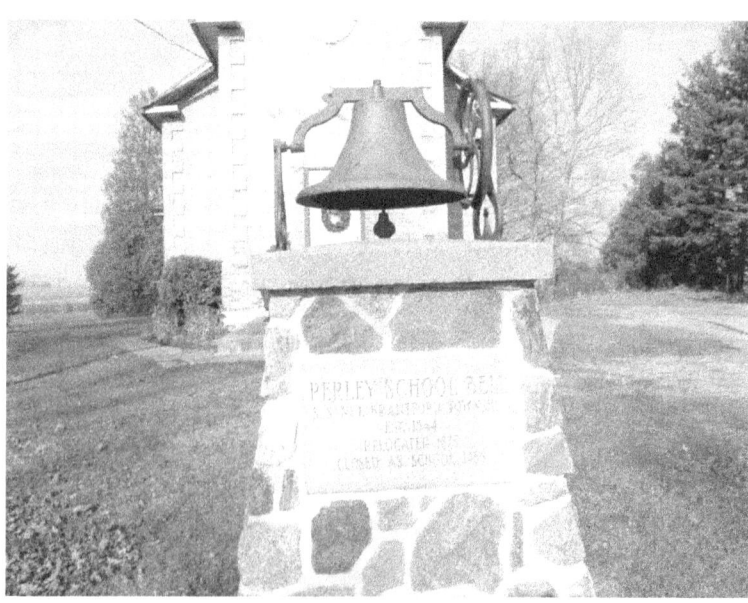

Perley School Bell
S.S. No. 1 Brantford Township
Established 1844, relocated 1875, closed as a school 1966

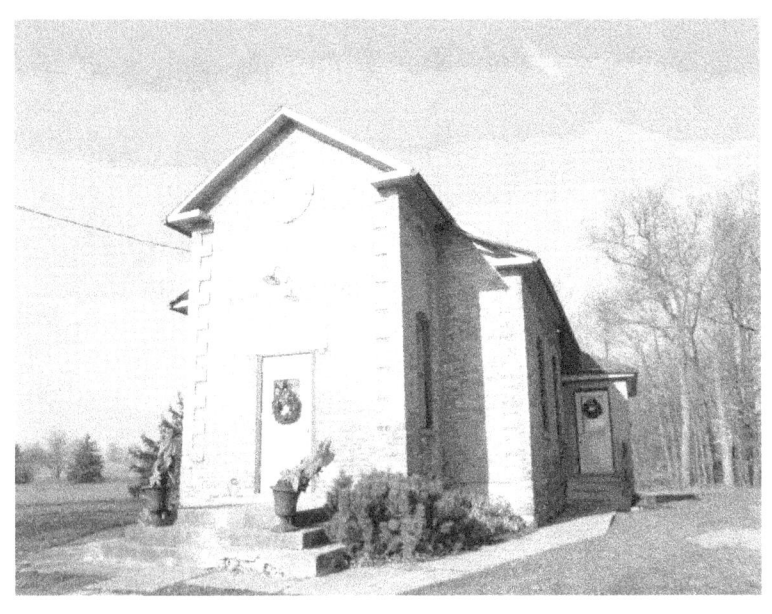

Bethel Community Centre

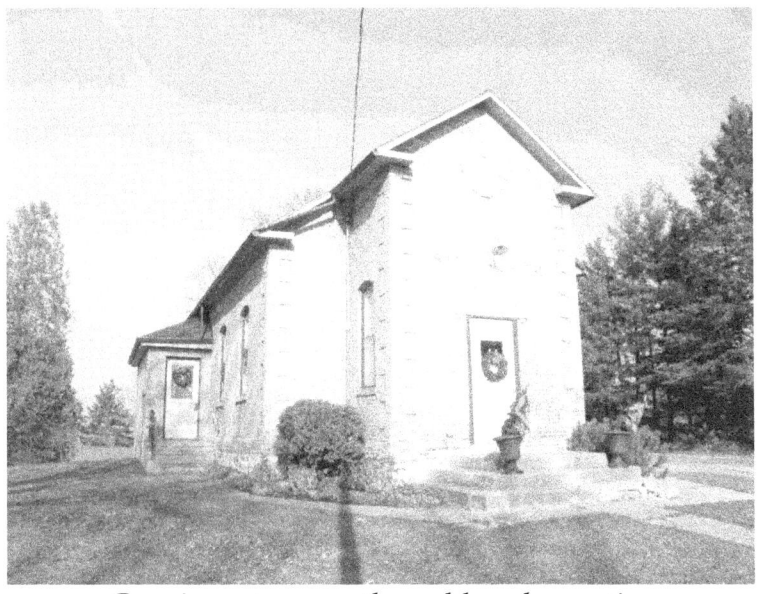

Cornice return on the gable - decorative

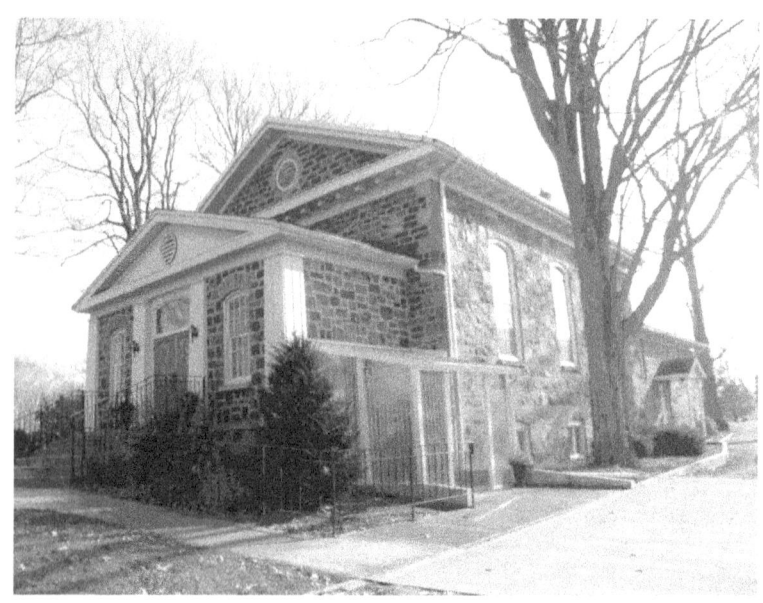

Bethel Stone United Church, 154 Bethel Road
(Methodist Church A.D. 1881)

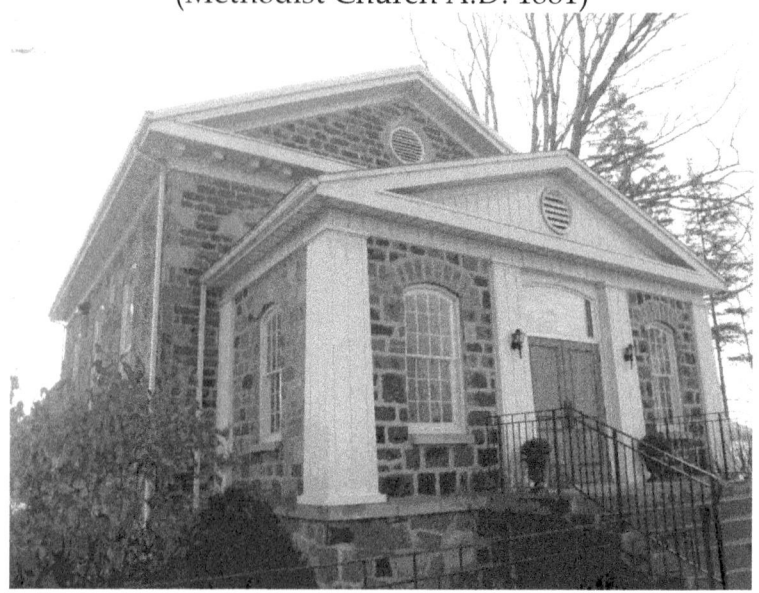

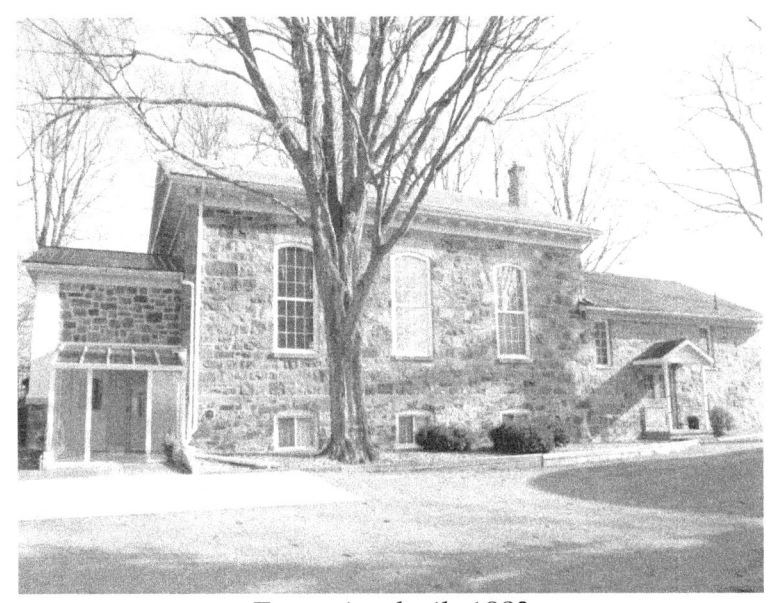

Extension built 1983

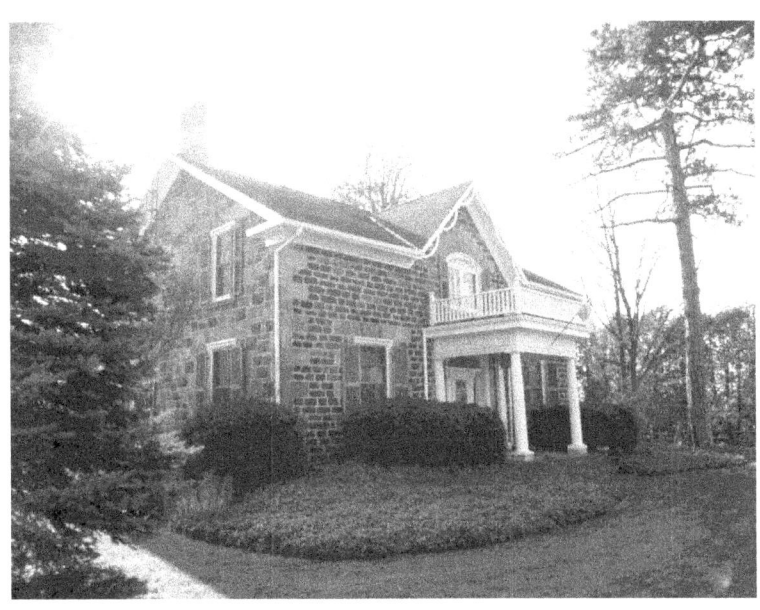

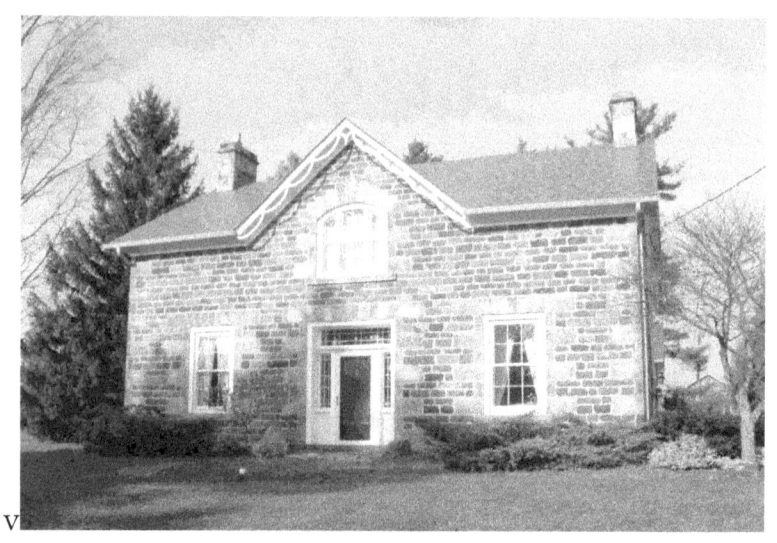

v

Macland Century Farm

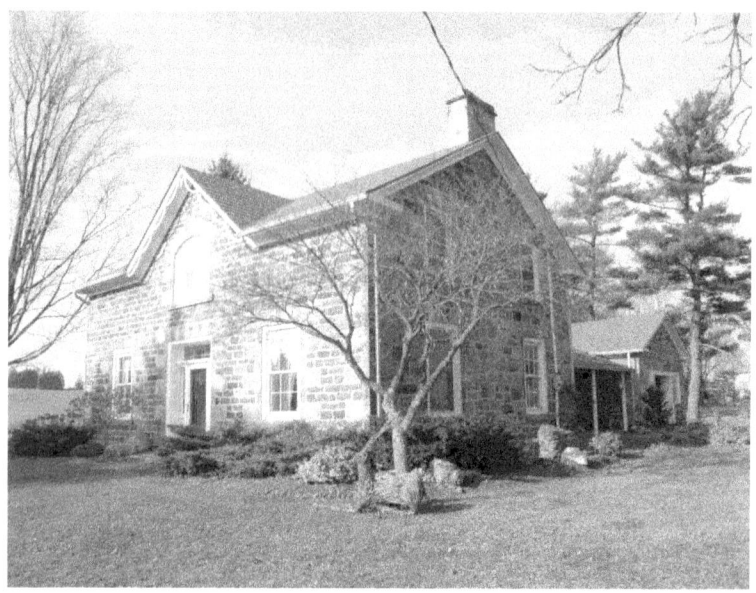

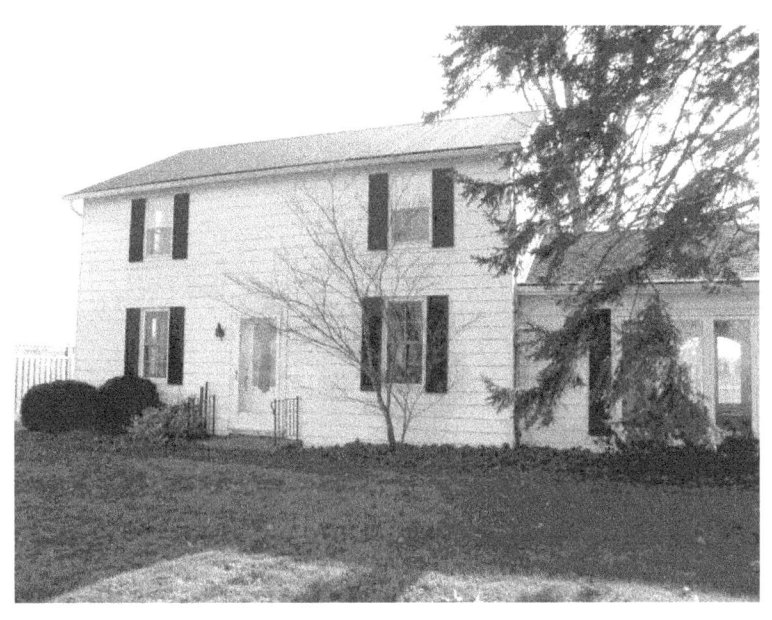

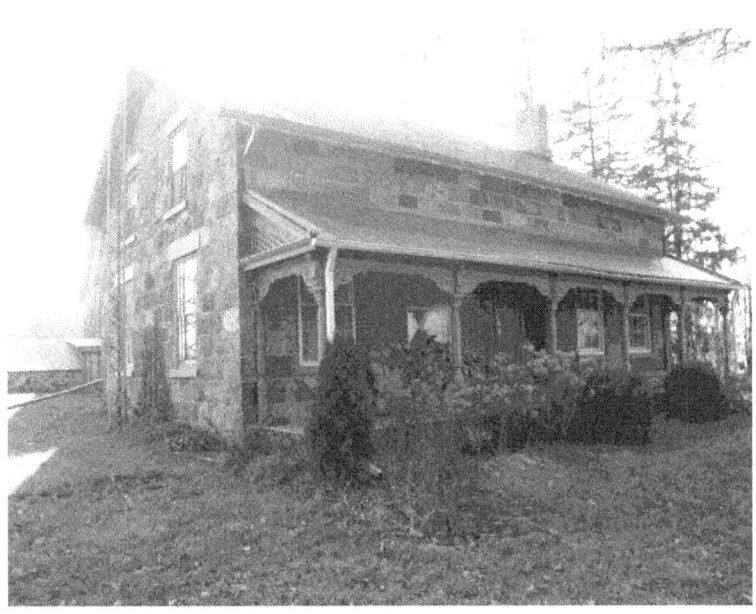

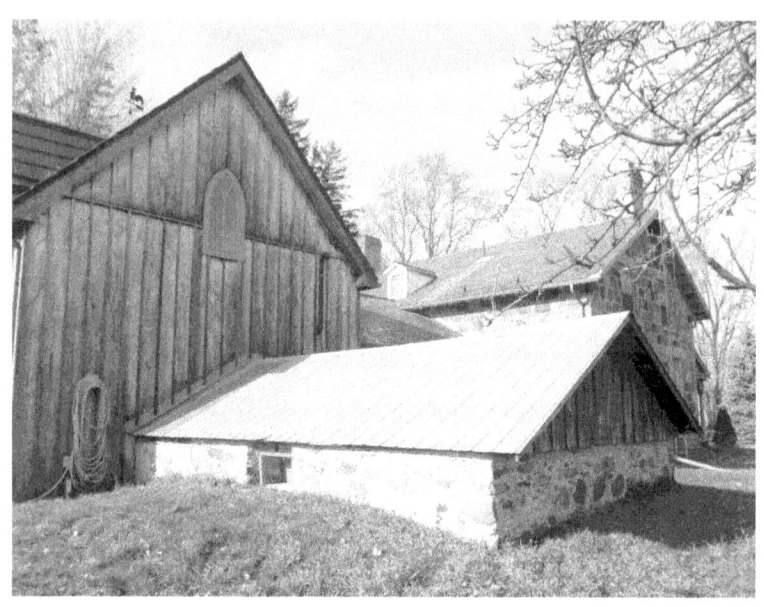

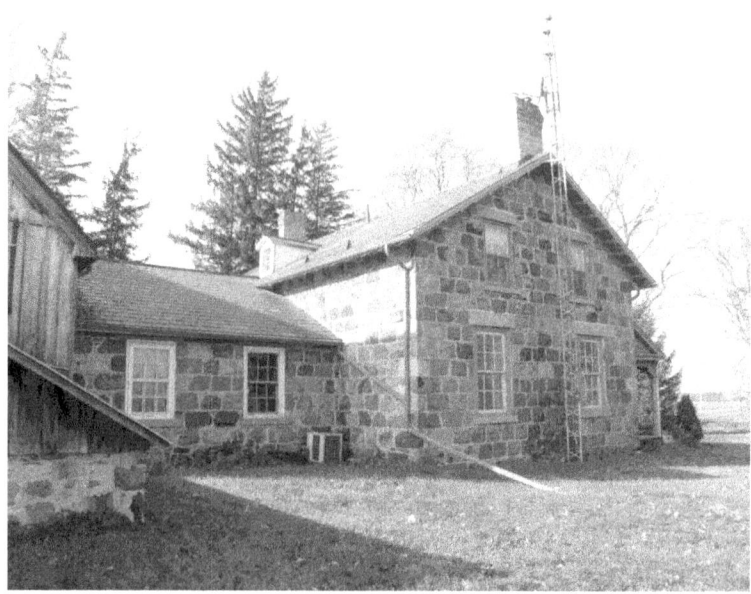

Multi-coloured stone

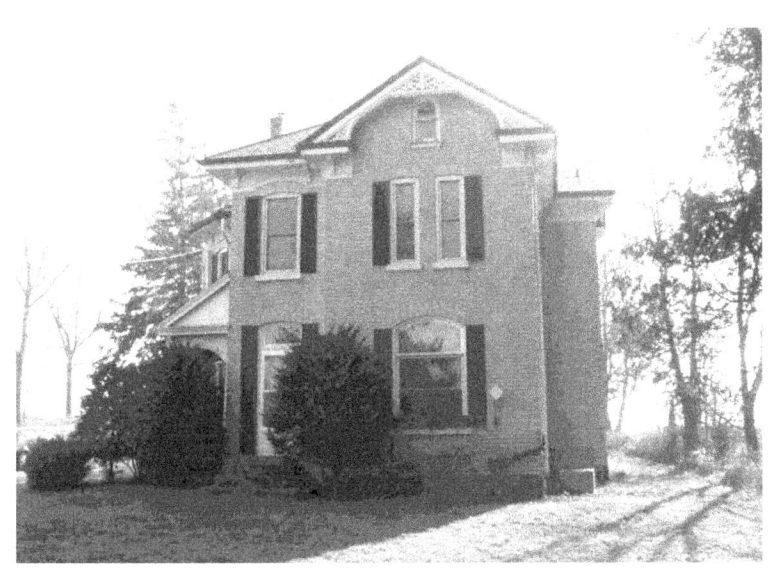

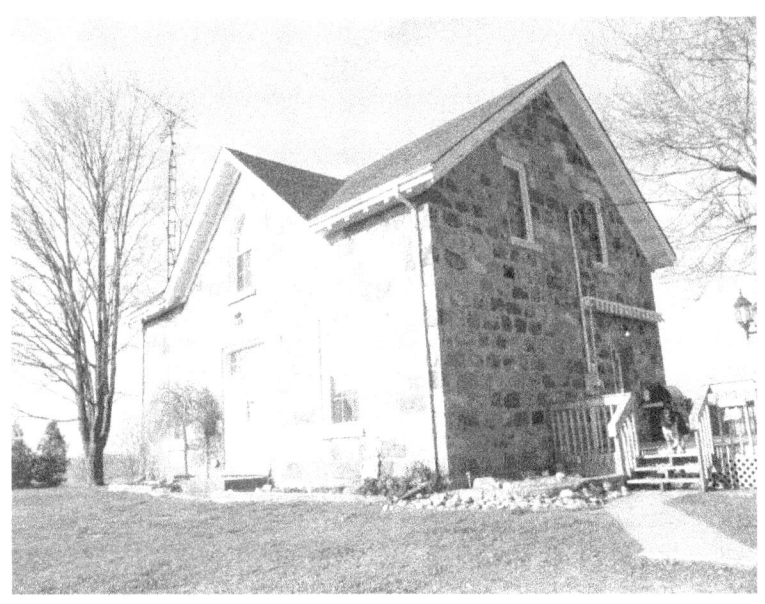

Falkland

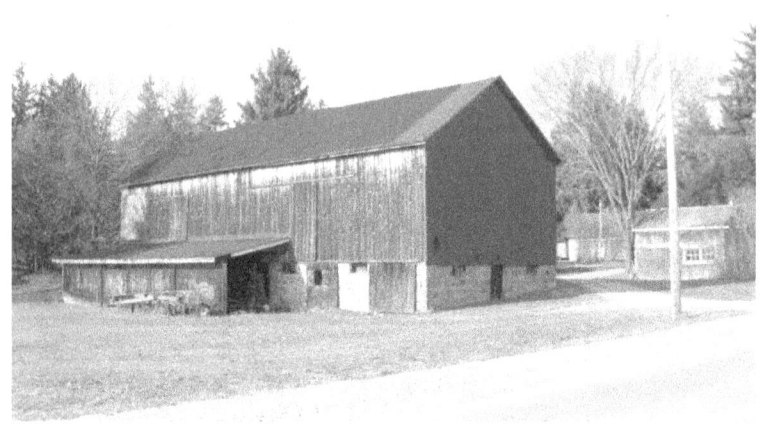

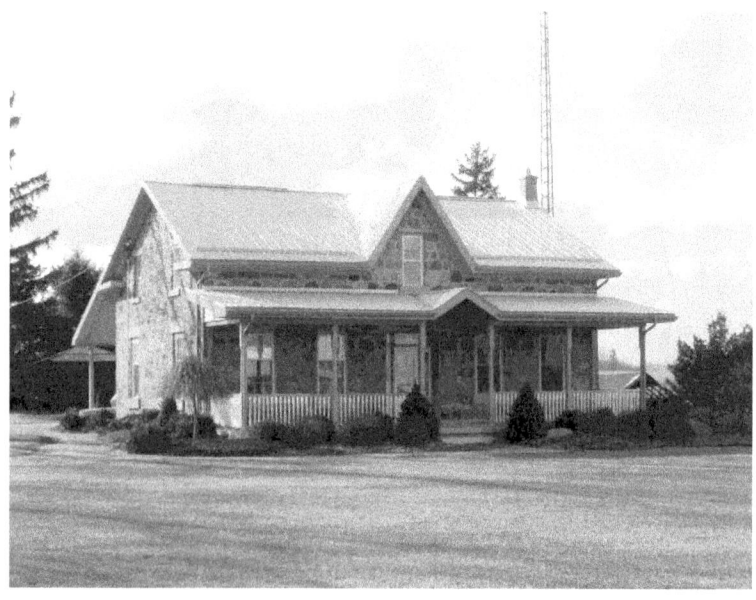

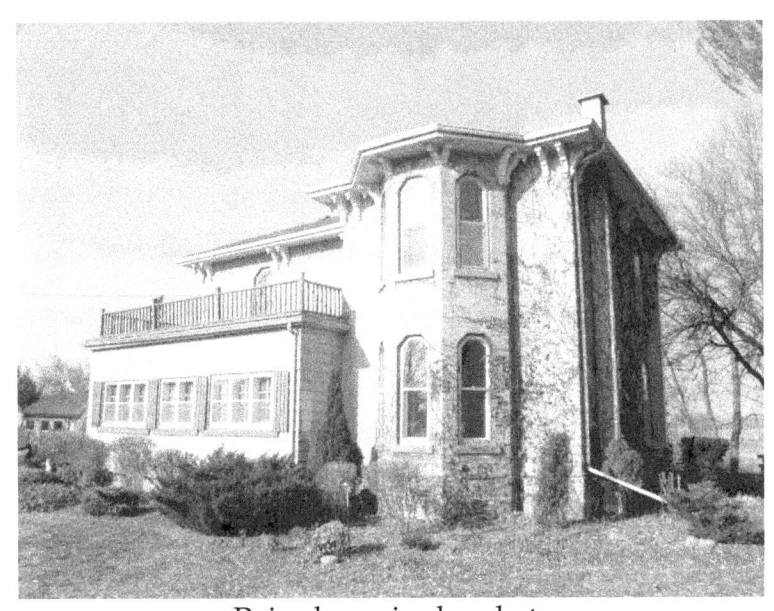

Paired cornice brackets

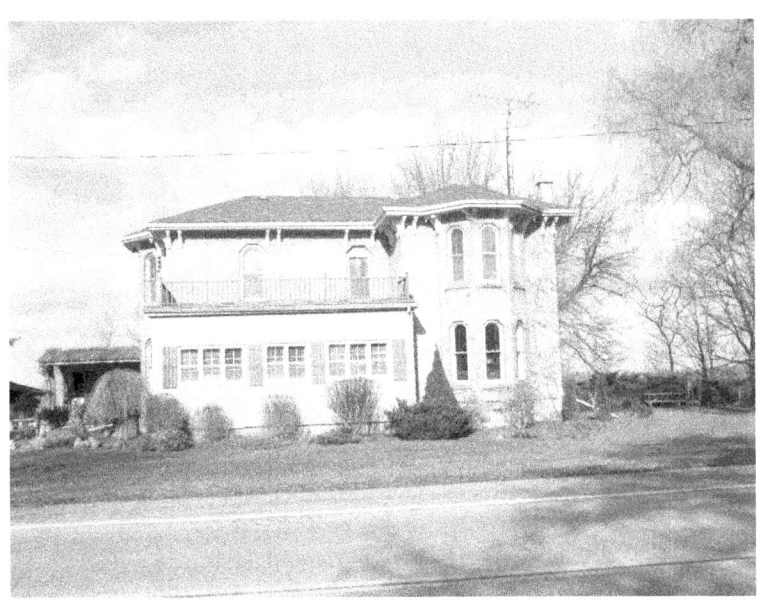

Eastwood

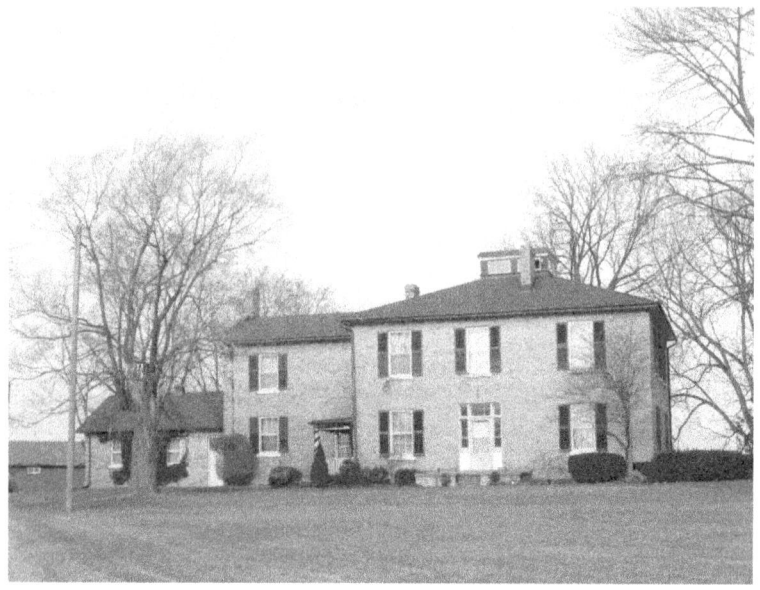

Etonia

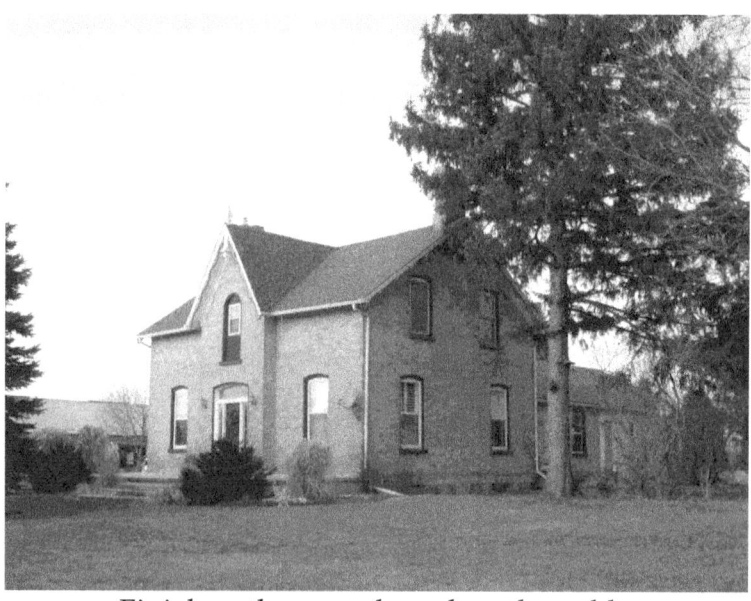

Finial on the vergeborad on the gable

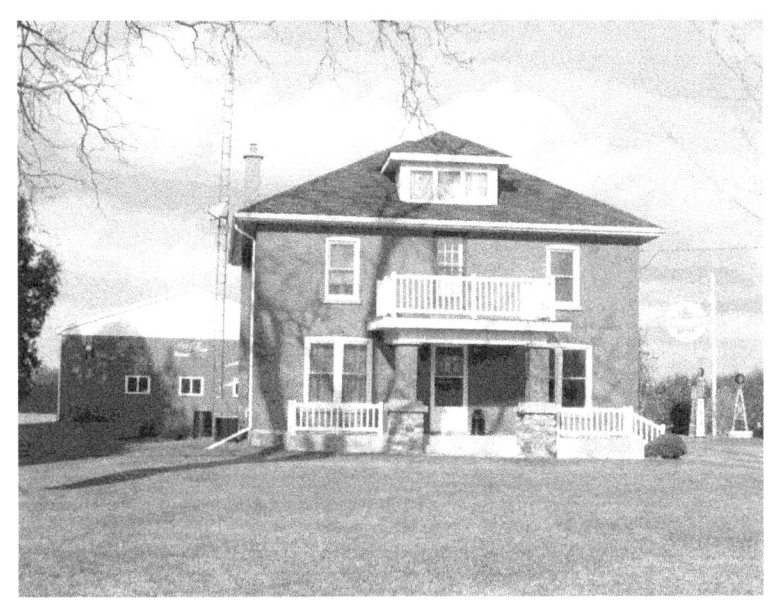

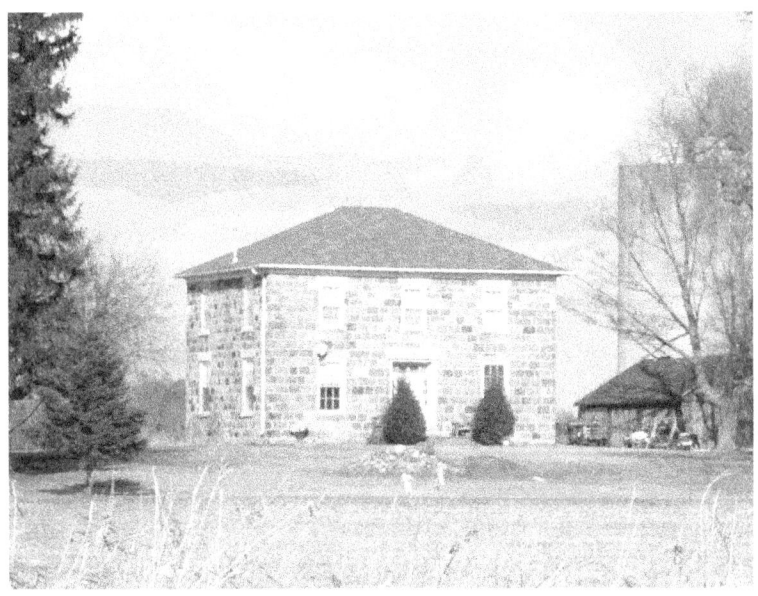

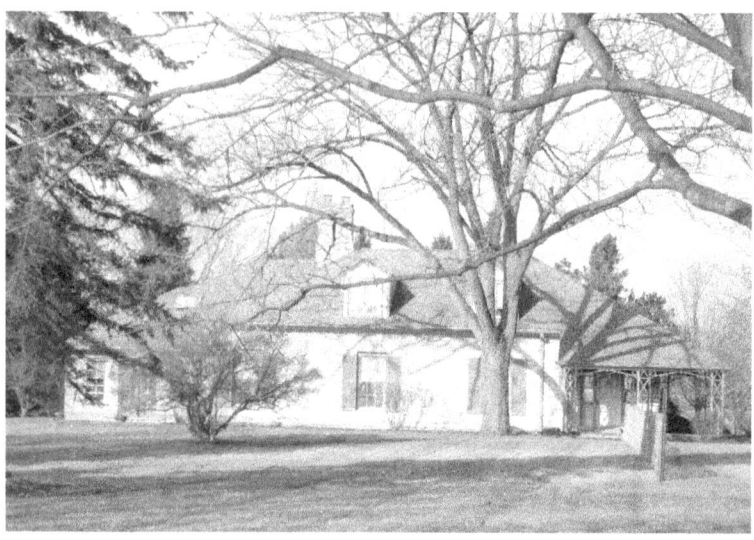

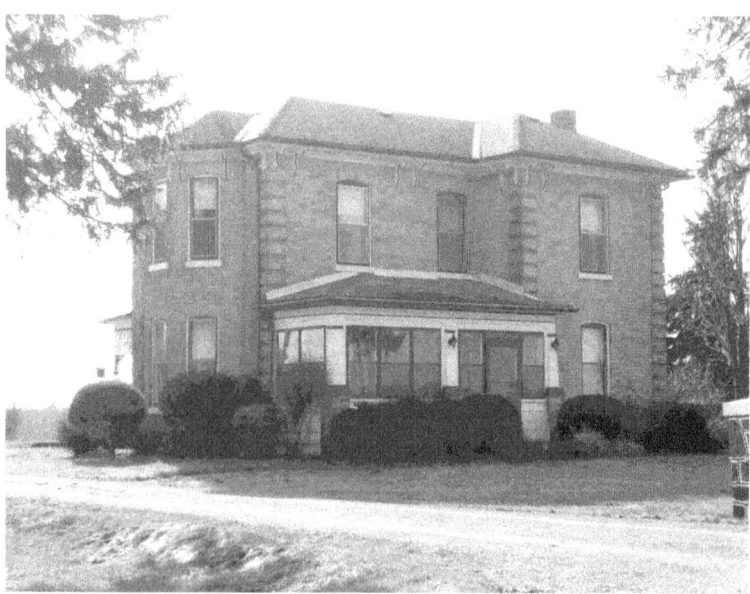

Paired cornice brackets, two-tone brick on corners

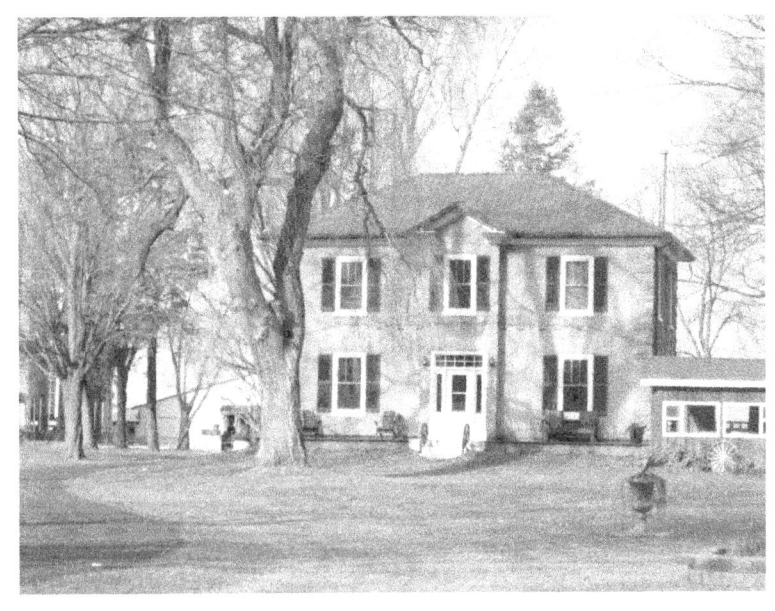

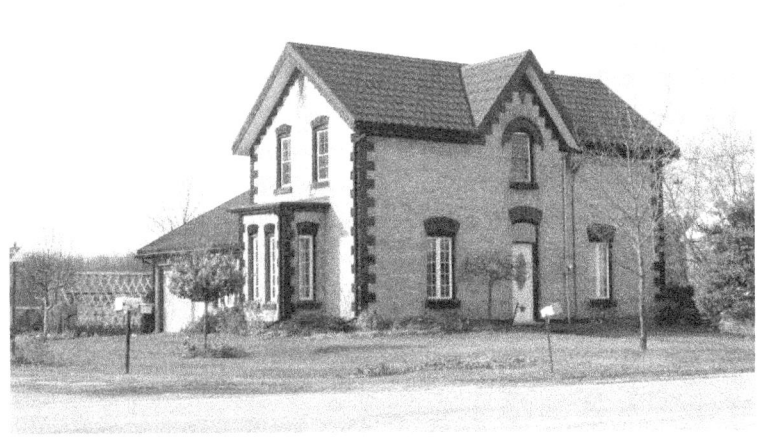

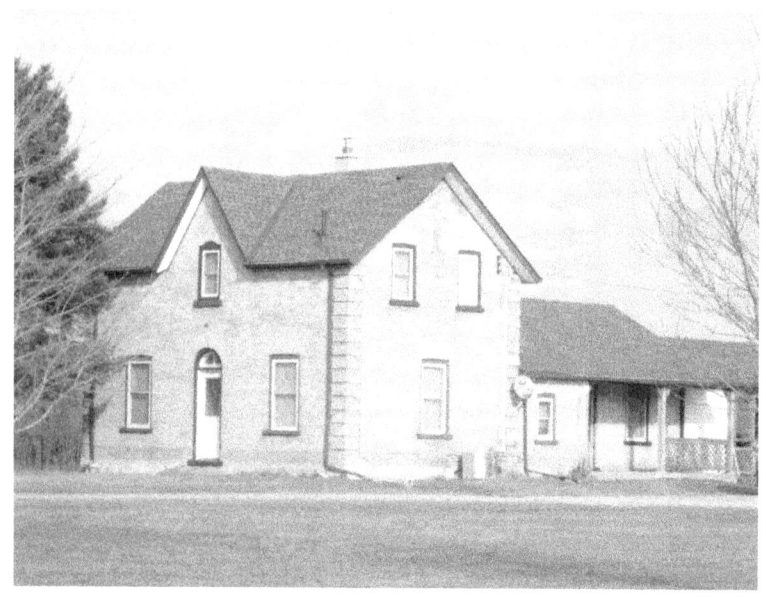

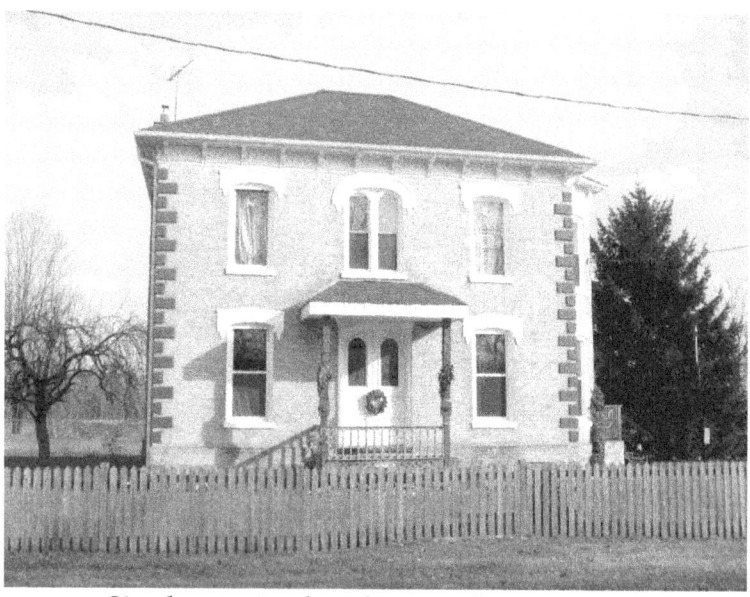

Single cornice brackets under the eaves
Two-tone brickwork on the corners, trim above the windows

Shakespeare

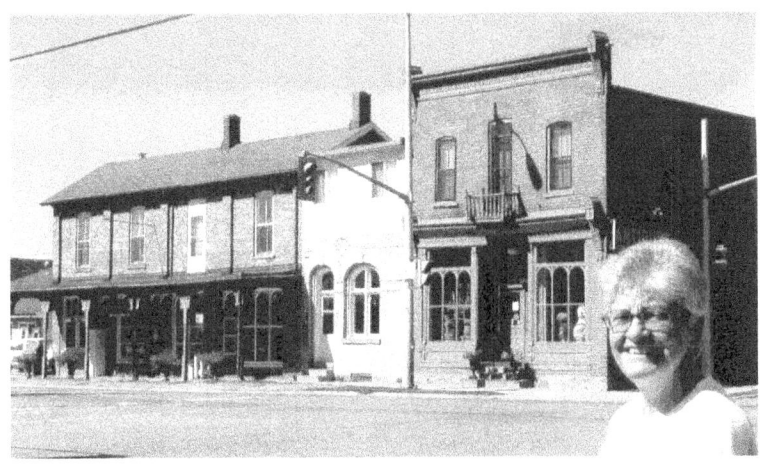

www.ingramcontent.com/pod-product-compliance
Lightning Source LLC
Chambersburg PA
CBHW051241170526
45165CB00004B/1519